The Sophia Teachings

The Sophia Teachings
The Emergence of the Divine Feminine in Our Time

Robert Powell

Lantern Books • New York
A Division of Booklight Inc.

2001
Lantern Books
One Union Square West, Suite 201
New York, NY 10003

Copyright © Robert Powell 2001

Printed in the United States of America

Library of Congress Cataloging-in-Publication Data

Powell, Robert
    The Sophia Teachings : the emergence of the divine feminine in our time / Robert Powell.
    p. cm.
ISBN 1-930051-52-2
    1.Wisdom—Religious aspects. I. Title.

BL65.W57 P69 2001
299'.93.—dc21
                                                            2001029795

Table of Contents

Introduction 1
1: The Divine Plan of Creation 11
2: Sophia in Ancient Greece 23
3: Why Sophia Disappeared from Western Culture 39
4: The Influence of Divine Sophia
   in the Western Mystical Tradition 53
5: The Influence of Divine Sophia in the East 79
6: Modern Teachings of Sophia 99
7: Reincarnation and the Second Coming 109
8: Other Traditions 135
9: The Age of Pisces and the Age of Aquarius 157
Epilogue 165

Acknowledgments

THIS BOOK WAS ORIGINALLY PUBLISHED AS THE six-tape set, *The Sophia Teachings*, recorded by Sounds True in Boulder, Colorado, for which I am indebted to Tami Simon and Michael Taft. Heartfelt gratitude to publisher Gene Gollogly for the inspiration to bring *The Sophia Teachings* into book form, to Carol Dunn of Lantern Books for her fine editing of the spoken text, to Rosamund Hughes who transcribed the tapes, and to Lacquanna Paul for accompanying *The Sophia Teachings* from beginning to end with encouragement and helpful suggestions.

Introduction

I FIRST CAME TO DIVINE SOPHIA THROUGH A
meeting with Eva Cliteur at the beginning of 1978. She had
invited me to Amsterdam to learn about her spiritual teacher, a
Russian individual whom I never met but who interestingly enough
had lived in the town in England where I grew up after he had left
Russia. His name was Valentin Tomberg and I had come across his
writings and became deeply interested in him. I wrote to Eva and we
planned to meet: It was really a turning point in my life. Eva provided
me with the background necessary for understanding Tomberg's life.
At the end of our meeting, she gave me a manuscript written in
French. "You are the one to translate this into English," she said.

At the time, I was about to go to Switzerland to begin a four-year
study in eurythmy—a spiritually based form of movement taught by
the Austrian esotericist Rudolf Steiner early in the twentieth century.
Nevertheless, I agreed to translate the manuscript and began work on

it. The process of translating took me through many experiences that awoke within me a relationship to the Divine Sophia. Through my experience with the manuscript, I was transformed from a mere translator into someone on a quest. I now believe that Sophia is someone who enables us to begin to discover who we are, what we think, what we feel, and what we are able to do, on a much deeper level than we can possibly imagine.

I shall go in to this in more detail; but from the outset I want to make clear that my spiritual awakening, my opening of the heart, my learning to think, and my beginning to feel in a new way opened up to me a multidimensional rather than a linear approach to things such as I had learned previously as a scientist and mathematician. I believe that we, as a society, lack these qualities. We have forgotten the ability to appreciate multidimensional aspects of existence. Through our scientific technological civilization we have lost this heart-felt relationship to existence and we need to find it again. Sophia is the one who can help us to do this. Sophia is the being who can open us up, who can breathe into us new life and warmth, new love and new appreciation for all that is around us. In communicating these Sophia teachings, I hope to be able to express something of this wonder, glory, and beauty that we can discover through finding Sophia.

What do I mean when I talk about "Sophia"? Fundamentally, I am not talking about an abstract quality such as "Wisdom"—the literal translation of the Greek word *Sophia*. In using the word Sophia, I am referring to a living being, a being who is the Divine Mother of humanity, one who cares for every one of us, who is deeply concerned about what is taking place in the world at the present time, and who is now drawing closer to humanity at this time of crisis. Sophia is a being who through immense love for every human being on this planet is concerned with finding a way out of the impasse into which we have come.

The manuscript I translated was eventually published as *Meditations on the Tarot: A Journey into Christian Hermeticism*. This work was written anonymously, to be published posthumously—mainly because the author, who lived from 1900 to 1973, wanted to communicate with us, the readers, as a friend who has gone on to live in another dimension of existence, and who from this other dimension is seeking to guide us. According to *Meditations*, there are three primary aspects of our relationship to existence. These are what we could call a mystical relationship to the world, a gnostic relationship to the world, and a magical relationship to the world. I will describe these briefly and then illustrate them in relationship to the Divine Sophia by referring to King Solomon, whom we could think of as an archetypal seeker of divine wisdom.

The Three Primary Aspects of Our Relationship to Existence

A mystical relationship to existence implies an opening of the heart. It is when a breath of divine love enters us. When this happens, we find that our whole feeling life becomes elevated and transformed and that we begin to find a much deeper level of relating to and feeling for the world than we can imagine in the normal course of life. Divine mysticism is something about which all the great mystics have spoken. Such a relationship is essential if we want to open to Sophia. We have to take the step from just feeling about things in an ordinary way to expanding our whole sensory and emotional life, if we are to start to feel a sense of divine union. This is a first step in finding a relationship to Divine Sophia. Throughout the book, I shall describe how prayer, meditation, and devotional practices can expand and open our feeling life into a mystical dimension.

The gnostic relationship to the world is expressed as a revelation of divine wisdom—that everything we see around us is actually a work of wisdom. This means that everything—even every flower—is a work of divine wisdom. What I mean by gnostic—which comes from the Greek word *gnosis* or knowledge—is a knowing on a deeper level than an abstract level of knowledge can possibly convey to us, one that has a quality of light and clarity that speaks to us from divine realms. In order to experience this kind of relationship we have to open our minds to divine wisdom, receive an inflowing of light, and begin to experience a living power of thought. This involves an elevation of our whole mental ability—in order to receive another dimension of existence into oneself. This kind of knowing is familiar to us from the whole tradition of philosophy. "Philosophy" or *Philos-Sophia* means "love of Sophia," and the first Greek philosophers truly loved Sophia and opened their minds to divine wisdom. This gnostic aspect speaks to us of the opening of our minds, just as a mystical aspect has to do with the opening of our hearts.

The magical aspect of this relationship involves the endeavor of aligning our own will with that of the divine, in service of the good, the true, and the beautiful. Divine or sacred magic means that our own will opens to become empowered by divine will. Again, I will refer to practices later that can help imbue our will with the higher spiritual power of sacred magic.

The three levels of relating to existence—mystical, gnostic, and magical—are the essence of what was communicated and opened up to me through work on translating *Meditations on the Tarot*. If we are able to embrace all three of these levels—the heart, the mind, and the will—we will become whole human beings in our mental life, our feeling life, and in our actions. This book aims to explore the exciting challenge of opening up to the Divine Sophia, who can address us on all three levels—through our minds, hearts, and will.

The transformation of my life did not end with my translation of the book. I had another experience that changed my life. It was two years later, in 1980, and also in Amsterdam. I visited a little chapel the manuscript had talked about. It had been built following a series of appearances by the Virgin Mary in Amsterdam, beginning in 1945 and continuing through 1959. In these appearances, Mary revealed herself to a woman under the title of the Lady of all Nations or Peoples. The chapel was built as a monument to the Virgin Mary for her seekers. At the chapel, I had a profound experience, through Mary, that led me to want to dedicate my life to the service of Sophia. After the experience at the chapel, it became clearer and clearer to me over time that there was a relationship between Mary and Sophia, that the Virgin Mary was in a sense a very high incarnation and embodiment of the Divine Sophia. This I will come back to later.

The Wisdom of Solomon
Throughout the course of history, Sophia—as the mother of humanity, or the guide who unfolds evolution—has revealed herself over and over again to different peoples with different traditions and religions. Her presence is ubiquitous in the major spiritual traditions and religions of the world. While I cannot hope to encompass all facets of Divine Sophia in this book, I can at least focus mainly on what we might call the Western Sophia tradition. However, I will also discuss elements of the Sophia traditions in Taoism, Buddhism, and Hinduism, as well as Judaism and Christianity.

The ancient provenance of Sophia is most dramatically and strikingly portrayed in the extraordinary revelations of Sophia we find in the Hebrew Bible in the life of King Solomon. We remember King Solomon for building a majestic temple about one thousand years before Christ. As we can learn through the Wisdom Books of the Hebrew Bible, Solomon was guided and helped in building this glorious temple by the inspiration of Divine Sophia. If we look at King Solomon as an archetypal seeker of wisdom, of Divine Sophia, we can see how he was connected with Sophia in a mystical, gnostic, and magical way. He was connected in a magical way through the building of the Temple, in a mystical way through his profound love and devotion for Divine Sophia, and in a gnostic way through the extraordinary illumination and guidance that he received from Divine Sophia.

Born the son of King David, the young Solomon was faced with a choice between riches, health, and wisdom. He chose wisdom. As it says in the Book of Kings:

> *God gave Solomon wisdom and understanding beyond measure and breadth of mind like the sand on the sea shore, so that Solomon's wisdom surpassed the wisdom of all the peoples of the East, and all the wisdom of Egypt, for he was wiser than all others.*

Solomon's profound wisdom was the result of his relationship with Sophia, which as I have suggested was a threefold relationship. The mystical relationship of Solomon with Divine Wisdom is expressed in the following words:

I loved Sophia and sought her out from my youth.
I sought to take her for my bride.
I became enamored of her beauty.
When I come into my house I find rest with her.
For converse with her has no bitterness,
And to live with her has no pain, but gladness and joy,
And in assiduous communion with her is understanding.

Here Solomon expresses his profound love of and deep feeling for Divine Sophia. She became for him a mystical bride, one who accompanied him from the other side of existence, from the spiritual realms. Clearly Solomon rejoiced in the glory of God's creation, and he opened his heart to Sophia, the wisdom of creation.

Now a skeptic might ask: How can this be possible? It is possible through prayer, meditation, and through simply becoming more and more attentive to the world around us. As I have suggested, every flower, tree, mountain, and lake can speak to us of Divine Sophia, of the love that weaves through the world, and to which our own hearts can open and respond. Through prayer and meditation and an open attentiveness, we can begin a conversation with the world—one conducted on the level of the heart. Such a conversation opens the way to a mystical union with Divine Sophia, such as Solomon enjoyed.

While Solomon was gifted with a profound love and appreciation of all that he took in from the world around him, his abilities are not confined only to him. We all have the ability to open our hearts to the glory of creation and the majesty of divine wisdom. We need only look up at the stars in the heavens on a clear night and see their incredible majesty and beauty and how the stars shine down upon us to begin to open our hearts to this realm. Mysticism is not something confined to a few great people. It is our God-given inheritance to appreciate the world through our hearts, to open ourselves to everything, and allow the experience to begin to speak in a profound way.

The openness is not only of the heart but, as I have suggested, of the mind. This is what I call the gnostic aspect of a deepened relationship to the world through opening to divine knowledge and understanding. In the case of Solomon, he received divine knowledge and understanding directly from Sophia. As he says in the Book of Wisdom:

> *A knowledge of the structure of the world, and the operation of the elements, the beginning and end of epochs, and their middle course, the alternating solstices and changing seasons, the cycles of the years and the constellations, the nature of living creatures and the behavior of wild beasts, the violent force of winds and human thought, the varieties of plants and the virtues of roots, I learned it all, hidden or manifest, for I was taught by Sophia, by her whose skill made all things.*

In these words of Solomon we see the possibility of receiving illumination from Divine Sophia, of receiving the light of wisdom and understanding. This also is a God-given inheritance. Every human being can through this opening of the mind begin to know on a higher level than any level of abstract knowledge. We can understand the world around us, penetrate the veil of appearances, and understand that there is wisdom and guidance behind all the phenomena of existence. Such an impulse to push through to the deeper laws of existence motivates every scientist. It is an impulse shared by us all: to pierce beyond the veil of appearances and discover the order and grandeur of existence. What Solomon's words illustrate is that there are divine laws that order the world around us. Even in seemingly unrelated, chaotic events, there is a profound wisdom. The movement of the clouds, the occurrences of the weather, all the phenomena of nature, are all expressions of wisdom. This is the wisdom of gnosis or divine knowledge.

Beyond the opening of our hearts and minds there is also the possibility of serving the divine—of aligning our own will with the higher will. To illustrate what we can understand from this, let us again look at King Solomon in his building of the Temple. The Temple can be defined as a work of sacred magic—where magic is conceived of as the alignment of human will with divine will. In the Book of Wisdom we find a prayer of King Solomon, which reveals this mystery of sacred magic:

You told me to build a temple on your sacred mountain, and an altar in the city which is your dwelling-place, a copy of the sacred tabernacle prepared by you from the beginning.

With you is Sophia, who is familiar with your works, and was present when you created the universe, who is aware of what is acceptable to you, and in keeping with your commandments.

Send her forth from your holy heaven, and from your glorious throne bid her come down so that she may labor at my side, and I may learn what is pleasing to you.

She knows and understands all things.

She will guide me prudently in whatever I do, and guard me with her glory.

Solomon's prayer tells us how the king turned to Divine Sophia for help in building the Temple, and how Sophia poured out her guidance and her blessing so that he was able to draw up his plan for this great construction. For Solomon, the Temple was to be a manifestation of divine will, an inspiring work here on Earth where every human being who entered it would have their inner life elevated and become aware of the mystery of the divine. The Temple of Solomon was a unique and majestic work of divine magic and a testimony to divine wisdom and love.

Once again, the faculty of divine magic is one we all have. If we open our hearts and minds, we can align our will with the divine will, and, through this, find a new relationship to the unfolding of life. Obviously, not all of us will be called to build a temple as Solomon was. But each one of us has a part to play in the unfolding plan of evolution, and we each have the potential to align our will with that of the divine. This is the work of sacred magic and this is an aspect of the new revelation of Sophia in our time—that we align ourselves with her and her unfolding of divine wisdom in the service of divine love for the fulfillment of the divine plan.

Of course, we need to know what the divine plan is. This means opening up to Sophia to receive her light of inspiration, the warmth of her being, and her guidance. Just as King Solomon received the light of Sophia, opened his heart to her, and was guided by her in his work as the king of Israel, so we can take this as a wonderful example, an archetype for each one of us to find a relationship to Sophia in our time when, as I believe, a new revelation of Sophia is beginning to unfold.

Chapter One
The Divine Plan of Creation

T HE DIVINE PLAN OF CREATION IS NOTHING
less than Sophia herself. If we open ourselves to what is
conveyed in the Books of Wisdom attributed to Solomon,
we find Sophia herself speaking as the wisdom of the creation. Here
are a few examples from Proverbs:

> *The Lord created me, the first of his works long ago, before all*
> *else that he made. I was formed in earliest times, at the*
> *beginning, before the Earth itself.*
>
> *I was born when there was yet no ocean, when there were*
> *no springs brimming with water.*
>
> *When he set the heavens in place, I was there.*
>
> *When he girdled the ocean with the horizon, when he fixed*
> *the canopy of clouds overhead, and confined the springs of the*
> *deep, then I was at his side each day, his beloved and delight,*

*rejoicing in his presence continually, rejoicing over the whole
world, while my delight was in humankind.*

Here Divine Sophia is described as being present from the
beginning of the creation. The one we call the Creator, in taking the
first step in the work of creation, called forth Sophia, divine wisdom,
as the plan of creation. In this way, Sophia is the embodiment of the
plan of creation. It is a plan where, as the Book of Proverbs cites,
Wisdom has built her house. She has set up her seven pillars—seven
pillars of creation, seven pillars in the temple of Divine Sophia. These
we can conceive of as seven stages in the unfolding of creation. I will
talk about these seven pillars, or the seven stages of creation, later on
in this book.

When I was in the chapel dedicated to the Lady of all Peoples in
Amsterdam, I was touched and moved to the depths of my being as I
experienced through Mary the Divine Sophia. We can imagine an
experience such as this in the life of King Solomon—except that
Solomon was touched and moved by Sophia not just at one point in
his life, but all the time. He had attained a degree of mystical, gnostic,
and magical union with Sophia such that she was present throughout
his life.

It should be noted here that the Wisdom Books attributed to
King Solomon reveal something about Sophia's teachings at that
particular time. The teachings were directed to the Children of Israel
at a specific moment in their history. Yet, if we look at the work of
Sophia in the unfolding of the history of humanity, we find that her
message of revelation is different at different times, according to the
people she is addressing. In the case of Solomon, some three thousand
years ago, the revelation occurred when the Temple was to be built to

house the tabernacle and to be a focus for the people of Israel in preparation for the coming of the Messiah. Here are a few passages from Proverbs that can communicate to us something of Sophia's teachings at that time. One quality that Sophia emphasizes frequently is justice, or righteousness.

> *I am wisdom. I bestow shrewdness and show the way to knowledge and discretion.*
>
> *From me come advice and ability. Understanding and power am I.*
>
> *Through me kings hold sway and governors enact just laws. Through me princes wield authority. From me all rulers on Earth derive their rank.*
>
> *Those who love me I love, and those who search for me will find me. I follow the course of justice and keep to the path of equity. I endow with riches those who love me.*

Sophia reveals herself as one who upholds justice and right-eousness—something that Sophia continually urges us to pursue. A modern example of this pursuit is Dr. Martin Luther King, Jr. who followed the path of nonviolence and offered up his life to help the cause of justice. I believe we could look upon Martin Luther King as one who was guided by Sophia. There are many other examples we could think of—Mahatma Gandhi in India, for instance, who upheld the path of justice and righteousness—so Divine Sophia can inspire all human beings who seek to fulfill what is just and righteous. This is one of the most important characteristics of the Sophia teachings as revealed by King Solomon. But there are other qualities as well. In the following passage from the Book of Wisdom we hear the magnificence of Sophia's being, of her various qualities, of the power and intelligence she is able to bestow on us when we turn toward her:

In Sophia there is a spirit intelligent and holy, unique in its kind, yet made up of many parts: subtle, free-moving, lucid, spotless, clear, neither harmed nor harming, loving what is good, eager, unhampered, beneficent, kindly towards all mortals, steadfast, unerring, untouched by care, all-powerful, all-surveying, and permeating every intelligent, pure, and most subtle spirit.

For wisdom moves more easily than motion itself. She is so pure she pervades and permeates all things. Like a fine mist she rises from the power of God, a clear effluence from the glory of the Almighty, so nothing defiled can enter into her by stealth. She is the radiance that streams from everlasting light, the flawless mirror of the active power of God, and the image of his goodness.

She is but one, yet can do all things. Herself unchanging, she makes all things new. Age after age she enters into holy souls, and makes them friends of God and prophets.

As described here, from age to age Sophia enters into holy souls and all those who seek her. She endows us with the wealth of her gifts, such as radiance, intelligence, love for beauty, and her powers of understanding. These are all qualities that holy human beings through the ages have manifested, and which are a testimony to the presence and the power of Sophia as active and guiding in the unfolding of humanity's evolution. When we think of the great teachers of humanity, of the enlightened ones, we think of Buddha in India, of Zarathustra in Persia, of Moses in Israel, and Hermes in

Egypt, and of individuals who were guided, moved, inspired, or filled by Divine Sophia. These are the great teachers of humanity, who have contributed something of an aspect of the being of Divine Sophia in helping to move humanity a step further in its evolution.

We learn from Solomon that Sophia is a divine being who can speak to us of the mystery of existence, of the wonder and glory of God's creation, and of all that radiates from every aspect of the creation. It is Sophia who opens up to us the mysteries of the seasons, of the relationships between Earth and the cosmos, the healing properties of plants and the mysteries of the animal kingdom, and the true relationship between humanity and the animal, plant, and mineral kingdoms. It is Sophia who reveals to us the properties of the different precious stones, what they convey to us, and their healing powers. All of this is a gift from Divine Sophia to humanity. Of course, Divine Sophia also casts her light of understanding upon the mysteries of human relationships.

In our time we have increasing need for the help and guidance of Divine Sophia. Modern science and technology have, through the computer and the Internet, brought the possibility of all human knowledge to us. Yet, the information superhighway conveys an enormous danger, if we are to remain content with human as opposed to divine knowledge. The task for each and every one of us, therefore, is to open up and develop our faculties and potential through spiritual work, prayer, and meditation. It is not a question simply of imbibing more and more knowledge, but of opening up our hearts and minds to the divine—something that goes beyond access to human knowledge. The danger inherent in the new, virtually unlimited access to human knowledge is that it can actually create a barrier to the opening-up to divine wisdom. This is especially true at the moment, when divine wisdom is beginning to draw closer and closer to humanity. I shall address this issue later in the book.

Divine wisdom goes beyond human knowledge. Divine wisdom has the potential to illumine our minds, to warm our hearts, to strengthen our will, and to make us truly human beings, whereas the acquisition of more and more knowledge will not do this. It can make us clever and intelligent, but it will not in itself open up our true humanity. Divine wisdom is concerned that we unfold our full potential as human beings. These qualities that I referred to earlier in quoting from the Books of Wisdom are the qualities that Divine Sophia is able to bestow upon us. In opening up to Sophia, we open up our own souls. We enter on a path of self-transformation, to become better, more worthy, human beings; to become servants of the good, the true, and the beautiful; to become more radiant human beings. And in King Solomon we see an archetype, a human being who, through opening himself up to Sophia, was able to accomplish great works a thousand years before Christ.

In the entire history of Israel we can sense something of the flowing-in of Divine Sophia in the quality of motherhood that was striven for by the women of Israel. This included a true sense for the values of family, motherhood, and a wish to be a bearer of wisdom. Eventually it culminated in the birth of the Virgin Mary, who represents the fulfillment of this impulse of perfect motherhood.

Demeter and Persephone
To bring out something of Sophia's role as the ideal of motherhood, I would like to refer to the story of Demeter and Persephone. Demeter, the goddess of fertility and the harvest, was worshiped in ancient Greece as Mother Earth. The word Demeter means simply Earth

Mother. Demeter had a daughter, Persephone, who was extremely beautiful. One day Persephone was walking in the fields with her maidservants picking flowers. Suddenly the earth opened up and Hades or Pluto, the god of the underworld, carried off Persephone into his domain. When Demeter learned of the disappearance of her daughter, she became filled with grief and set out to find her. This quality of love of a mother for her child comes through the inspiration of Divine Sophia. All this is part of a profound teaching, which we will go into later on.

Moved by her deep and profound love for her daughter, Demeter searched everywhere for Persephone. In her quest, she dressed up as an old woman, and eventually came to the home of the Keleos, king of Eleusis, where she was invited to become a nurse to the king's son, Demophon. Here we see again a mystery connected with the Divine Feminine, the mystery of education, of preparation, of helping the human being from the moment of birth on. For what did Demeter do? She took the child and each night she held this child in the flames of the fire in order to bestow immortality upon him. In this we can see something of the goal of divine wisdom, which is that all human beings will eventually become immortal.

Demeter, as the regent of all life here on Earth, was able to pour the fire of divine life into the limbs of this child. But one night, Metaneira, the queen of Eleusis, came down and saw Demeter holding the baby in the flames and became frightened, and at that moment Demeter's work of creating immortality was interrupted. The story goes that Demeter decided she would no longer bring forth the harvest, that famine would reign on Earth. Zeus, however, intervened, and sent down Hermes, the messenger of the gods, to plead with Hades, the lord of the underworld, to release Persephone. Hades agreed, but at the same time he broke his word when he gave a pomegranate to Persephone. Eating the pomegranate, Persephone took the seed of the underworld into herself, and was thus unable to be released from it completely. She had to spend part of the year with Hades in the underworld and the rest of the year was reunited with her mother Demeter in the upper world.

The story of Demeter and Persephone has many different levels of interpretation. On one level, Persephone represents the human soul who, through incarnating upon the Earth, falls from the divine world, becomes lost in the realm of darkness, and has to be found again. Demeter, the mother, as an aspect of the Divine Sophia, calls to the human soul to lead it back from the kingdom of darkness into the light of the world of spirit. This is one interpretation of the story, which is powerful because it communicates to us the love of Sophia, as the mother of all humanity, for each and every human soul. Any human being finding him- or herself in darkness or distress can turn to Sophia, the mother of humanity, for help in recovering their divine origin.

Another level of interpretation is that Demeter is the Divine Mother of everything, that she is Mother Earth, a living being, whose breath we can experience in the wind, whose circulation of blood we can experience in the movement of the streams, rivers, and ocean. She is the queen of all life here on the Earth. However, the source of her radiant life is found in the center of the Earth, so that all plants and trees grow down toward that center. The mystery teachings tell us that at the center of the Earth there is a golden realm, the kingdom of the Divine Mother. This is the kingdom known in the East as Shambhala, the lost paradise, which at the time of the Fall was lost and descended into the center of the Earth as a golden globe.

The story of Demeter and Persephone shows us that the Divine Feminine is also related to the center of the Earth and that Persephone, the daughter of Demeter, is actually an aspect of Demeter herself who descends into the depths. From those depths there radiates out the power of new life and the possibility of regeneration through establishing a relationship with the Earth Mother. We come to understand that the mysteries of the Divine Feminine, as represented in the story of Demeter and Persephone, have to do with profound secrets of evolution and the achievement of immortality. More importantly, it shows us that the Earth Mother is able to bestow immortality upon all of humanity if we find the right relationship to her. I shall explore this relationship in more detail later on.

The story of Demeter and Persephone reveals a wonderful outpouring of divine motherly love for the human soul, the culmination of which, in the human realm, we find in the relationship of the Virgin Mary to her son Jesus. We recall the guidance of Divine Sophia in the history of Israel to produce the perfect human being, and that the Virgin Mary fulfilled this role as the ideal mother. Just as Demeter was trying to bestow immortality upon the child at Eleusis, the Virgin Mary gave birth and was the mother of Jesus, a savior who attained immortality through the resurrection. What was present in the story of Demeter as myth we see actualized in the life of Christ. The Virgin Mary fulfilled the role of Divine Sophia toward Christ. This brings out a whole new aspect of the Sophia teachings, namely that in the Christian tradition the ultimate goal of spiritual evolution is to be found in the mystery of the resurrection. This was personally experienced by Jesus Christ two thousand years ago, and it stands as a sign that all human beings, through Christ, can achieve immortality through the resurrection.

So far we have looked at the example of King Solomon as an archetypal seeker of the Divine Feminine, and we have seen something of Sophia's work in the unfolding of evolution. We might therefore ask: What was Sophia's role in the ancient world? As divine wisdom, Sophia established her mystery centers within various religions and spiritual traditions in the ancient world. The mystery school at Eleusis honoring Demeter and Persephone is one example. There were definite rites of initiation, all of which were inspired by Divine Sophia through the archetypes of Demeter and Persephone. The mystery center at Eleusis was a source of inspiration for the Greeks and for other people who came from far and wide to experience something of these mysteries. Ancient writings make reference to the fact that for those who partook of these mysteries it was the most sublime experience of their lives. Of course, they were forbidden to speak about the actual content of these mysteries, but a few hints have come down to us. For example, the culmination in the mysteries of Demeter at Eleusis was the sublime experience of the emergence of the goddess, holding a child. We can see this as a prophetic announcement of that which later came to be fulfilled through the Virgin Mary with the child Jesus.

Another significant mystery center was established at Ephesus, where Artemis as an aspect of the Divine Sophia was worshiped. At Ephesus there was an extraordinary temple, one of the seven wonders of the ancient world, again built through the inspiration of divine wisdom. Inside the temple was a colossal cult statue of Artemis, and people came from throughout the Mediterranean and the Near East to be initiated into her mysteries. What, we may ask, was the content of initiation at Ephesus? We are told that those who entered the temple, after having prepared themselves, approached the cult statue

The Divine Plan of Creation

and, through a process of inner identification with Artemis, they became lifted out of themselves into an experience of the mysteries of the cosmos. They began to experience another, higher dimension of existence and to hear the inner sounds of the cosmos, or what is often called the music of the spheres. Alexander the Great was initiated in the temple at Ephesus, as were many of the great Greek philosophers, though some were initiated at Eleusis.

The goddess Isis represents another aspect of the Divine Feminine that was central to the mysteries of Egypt. Many of the magnificent temples in ancient Egypt were built as monuments to honor her divine wisdom, for it was she who brought the laws that governed the Egyptian people. Upon those who sought her, she bestowed the will to do good and serve the divine. The common theme among the great mystery schools of Isis in Egypt, Artemis in Ephesus, and Demeter and Persephone in Eleusis, shows that they were all part of the unfolding of Sophia's mysteries of the Divine Feminine in antiquity.

If we look at our present world, we see how impoverished we are through lack of turning to the Divine Feminine. As we stand at the beginning of the twenty-first century, it is important, even crucial, that the Divine Feminine become a new power of inspiration in human affairs. Sophia has the possibility of becoming a shaping influence for civilization as we unfold into the future. We are now entering a new era where Sophia is attempting to become more and more part of our lives, and this is the deeper meaning and significance of occupying ourselves now with the Sophia teachings. We are at a very important threshold, one that brings many challenges, and of course there are forces at work in the world to hinder this unfolding of the Divine Feminine. I believe that if we are open to her divine influence, Sophia can increasingly become our guide and continuing source of inspiration for all that we seek to do in our lives. And for every problem that we have in our lives, every question of destiny, we can turn to Sophia as a source of guidance, help, and inner strength.

Chapter Two
Sophia in Ancient Greece

THE TROJAN WAR WAS A VERY SIGNIFICANT moment in human evolution. To understand what it reveals to us of divine wisdom we need to know how the city of Troy came to be built. Legend tells us that one day Ilias, founder of the city of Troy, was asleep and had an extraordinary dream that the gods were communicating with him. When he woke up he found nearby a statue of a woman holding a shield and carrying a spear. It was a statue of the Greek goddess Pallas Athena. According to mythology Pallas, the companion of Athena, was killed in battle and Pallas Athena, therefore, represents the goddess Athena in her warlike aspect.

Greek mythology also tells us that Athena was a goddess of wisdom, born from the head of her father Zeus. The founding of Troy received the blessing of divine wisdom because Ilium built the city of Troy to house the sacred statue of Pallas Athena, the Palladium. It was said that whoever possessed the Palladium would have rulership of the world, and Troy possessed the Palladium. The Palladium was housed in a special underground temple guarded by vestal virgins. A sacred fire burned in this temple twenty-four hours a day, and this was the source and seat of the extraordinary power of the city of Troy. Scholars tell us that Troy, being located in Asia Minor, was the last citadel of ancient oriental wisdom where it reached its final crystallized form. And yet Troy, as the seat of wisdom, was not to remain invulnerable. This is what the Trojan War is all about.

How did the Trojan War begin? Priam was king of Troy around 1200 BCE, although we do not know the exact dates. He had fifty sons, one of whom was Paris. During her pregnancy, Paris' mother had a dream that with Paris the city of Troy would be destroyed. In order to avoid the fulfillment of this dream, Paris was sent as a small baby to grow up with shepherds on Mount Ida, some distance away from the city of Troy. Paris grew up there as a shepherd, a very beautiful young man, knowing nothing of his status as a prince of Troy. One day a quarrel broke out between the three goddesses—Hera, the wife of Zeus, goddess of power, Athena, goddess of wisdom, and Aphrodite, goddess of beauty—as to whom among them was the greatest. They agreed that a mortal should decide which of them was the greatest, and they chose Paris to resolve their quarrel. The three goddesses appeared to Paris on Mount Ida, presented him with a golden apple, and told him to give the golden apple to the goddess he thought was the greatest. Hera promised him conquest of many lands and undreamed of power; Athena promised him all the wisdom she could bestow on him; and Aphrodite promised to find him the most beautiful woman in the world. Paris handed the golden apple to Aphrodite, and she, therefore, had to fulfill her promise to find him the most beautiful woman in the world. This was Helen, the Greek wife of King Menelaus. Aphrodite visited Helen and caused her to fall in love with Paris, whom Aphrodite had also guided to visit the palace while Menelaus was absent. Paris abducted Helen, and sailed off with her to the city of Troy. So Helen, the most beautiful woman in the world, became known as Helen of Troy.

All of this points to a Sophianic theme, that the gift of Aphrodite, the gift of love, will one day ascend over the gift of power that is the gift of Hera and the gift of wisdom that is the gift of Athena. It is, therefore, a prophetic story.

The Greek kings were, of course, outraged at this event, and decided to take revenge by sailing to Troy and recapturing Helen. They raised a large army, set out on a great voyage, and besieged the city of Troy. They took with them their finest heroes, among them Achilles, who represents brute strength, and Odysseus, who represents cunning, wisdom, and intelligence. As we know from Homer's description, the Trojan War continued for ten years. It seemed that the Greeks simply could not capture the city of Troy owing to the fact that Troy possessed the Palladium. According to one version of the story, Odysseus, disguised as a beggar, came into the city and was able to capture and remove the Palladium. This was the first stage of the conquest of the city.

The next stage was that Odysseus thought of constructing the Trojan horse, a wooden horse huge enough to hide several Greek soldiers. A message was attached to the Trojan horse, saying, *Herewith the Greeks acknowledge the superiority of the Trojans, and bestow this horse as a present and return to their country.* The Greeks left the Trojan horse on the beach and they got into their ships and set sail, but withdrew only a short distance. When the Trojans came out of the city and saw this extraordinary present they wanted to bring the horse into the city. Despite warnings that this could be a trick on the part of the Greeks, the Trojans took the horse into the city. That night, the Greek soldiers, who were hidden in the belly of the horse, came out from their hiding place and began to slay the Trojans. Then they opened the city gates, so that the Greeks, who had in the meantime returned in their ships, were able to conquer the city and in this way recapture Helen.

In this story we find that divine wisdom became allied with the Greeks, especially in the figure of Odysseus, who represented a new faculty of intelligence. Here we see a symbolic transition from ancient Asian culture to the new and young culture of the Greeks. It points to the fact that the Greeks were to become the ascendant people, the vessel for the next stage of evolution, supported and guided by divine wisdom. Therefore, we can think of Sophia as the mother of both Greek and European civilization.

The rise of Greek culture and the founding of the Greek city-states took place under the inspiration of Athena, the goddess associated with the Palladium. Athena was also the inspiration of the Greek philosophers. We find the seven sages of ancient Greece arising in Asia Minor but really being the bearers of this new culture, which was characterized by active engagement of human thought and intelligence. In order to define this transition, we could say that ancient oriental civilization, up to and including the fall of Troy, was based not on the power of thought, but on what we could call ancient clairvoyance, a power of vision. Greek culture signified the transition from clairvoyance to rational thought.

Why did this transition need to take place? It has to do with the evolutionary plan that each human being become independent, and this is bound up with our ability to think. Through our ability to think, we are free and independent human beings. The ancient clairvoyance was a dreamlike kind of faculty that gave an ability to spiritually perceive events and behold the creative powers of existence reflected as the different gods and goddesses. This meant that human beings were subservient to the gods and goddesses, and were not really able to be free and independent beings in relationship to them. Human freedom came about precisely through the development of thinking.

Another Greek myth brings this out in a wonderful way. This is the myth of Perseus slaying Medusa. According to this Greek legend, Medusa had been at one time a beautiful woman. But during the course of time she developed snakes for hair, and anybody who looked at Medusa would be turned to stone. In this context, we might ask, what does Medusa really symbolize? I wish to argue that she is a depiction of the ancient power of clairvoyance, what in the East is called the power of the serpent, or the Kundalini. The snakes coming out of Medusa's head show this ancient force of clairvoyance gone wild and having become a danger, so that any human being exposed to this force could become paralyzed in their own being. They could become imprisoned through not having a free relationship to the visions arising through their clairvoyance. We can understand this if we recall that sometimes when we are dreaming we feel that events take place without our free initiative, and consequently we feel powerless. This analogy reveals something of the quality of this ancient clairvoyant faculty that all human beings possessed at that time.

In the legend of Perseus, the young Greek hero, who represents the new faculty of intelligence, decides he will slay Medusa. How is he going to do this when Medusa has such a terrifying appearance that just one look from her is sufficient to turn him to stone? Perseus is aided in his conquest of Medusa by Athena, goddess of wisdom. Here we see another indication that Athena, as an aspect of the Divine Sophia, was really behind the transition in evolution from clairvoyance to the development of human intelligence and thought. Athena accompanies Perseus to the domain of Medusa, and she holds up her shield so that Perseus can see the reflection of Medusa without looking at her directly. Walking backwards with the shield of Athena, Perseus engages in battle with Medusa and in his victory he cuts off her head. Here we see the application of intelligence to overcome the terrifying power of ancient clairvoyance.

The transition from ancient oriental clairvoyance to Greek rational thought is further highlighted in the legend of Andromeda and Perseus. Andromeda was the daughter of Cepheus and Cassiopeia, king and queen of Ethiopia. Their beautiful daughter Andromeda in a certain respect, like Helen of Troy, represents the soul of the world. Andromeda was dearly loved by Cepheus and Cassiopeia. However, a sea monster began to threaten the country, causing great destruction. An oracle revealed to the king and queen that the only way to save their country from destruction by the sea monster Cetus, who was like an enormous whale, was through the sacrifice of their daughter Andromeda. Symbolically the soul of humanity, represented by Andromeda, is being threatened by an atavistic force of the will, represented by the sea monster Cetus, a force from the depths. Through the constructive use of this atavistic force of the will, great structures such as the pyramids in Egypt and Stonehenge in the British Isles were built in antiquity. This constituted an enormous strength of will. But, just as ancient clairvoyance was a threat to the development of human freedom, so too this atavistic force of will was a threat to the development of independence. The task of saving Andromeda fell to Perseus. At the very moment when Andromeda was bound to a rock and was about to be devoured by Cetus, Perseus appeared holding the head of Medusa, and turned her evil eye upon Cetus. The sea monster was turned to stone. Here we see the use of intelligence to overcome the atavistic power of the will, all of this under the guidance and inspiration of Athena, the goddess of wisdom, an aspect of Divine Sophia. In the myth of Perseus we see the representative of the new Greek consciousness, as one who uses his intelligence and his power of thought in order to be guided through life.

Perseus, of course, is a mythological figure, whereas Odysseus, whom Homer tells us was the key figure in the conquest of the city of Troy through the use of intelligence, was an actual Greek personality. We know that the Trojan War actually took place, because the German archeologist Heinrich Schliemann was inspired and guided to the actual site where the Trojan War took place and was able to rediscover the city of Troy. In the story of the Greeks re-capturing Helen of Troy, representing the soul of humankind, in turn related to Divine Sophia, we see symbolically how the love of Sophia played an important part in the emergence of Greek civilization.

Pythagoras and the Greek Philosophers

One of the first Greek philosophers was Thales, who was born around 624 BCE. It was he who initiated the development of Greek philosophy around the start of the sixth century BCE that culminated centuries later with Plato and Aristotle. Thales contemplated deeply the origin of the world and the human being's relationship to it—a central question that occupied the Greek philosophers. Thales conceived of the world as having come into being from the substance of water, whereas Heraclitus of Ephesus conceived of the world as having originated through the power of fire, which he identified with the Logos. In this way, we can see that the Greek philosophers were really wrestling with these fundamental questions and did not necessarily arrive at the same conclusions. These Greek philosophers were inspired by Sophia, and through her divine wisdom human beings could begin to form a new relationship with Sophia through the use of the power of thought. This is what gave birth to philosophy. When we consider the original meaning of the word philosophy, *philosophia*, love of Sophia, we can see it was really love for the Divine Sophia, who was present from the beginning as the divine plan of creation, that gave birth to philosophy.

The philosopher Pythagoras was the first to call himself a philosopher and to actually use the expression philosophy. Because of this, I would like to focus briefly upon Pythagoras as a central figure in the Western Sophia tradition, a key figure who gathered together the threads of the ancient wisdom, carried them over into Greek culture, and founded a mystery school in Southern Italy.

Pythagoras was born in the first half of the sixth century BCE on the island of Samos, and travelled far and wide to gather wisdom from the different traditions of the ancient world. He visited Egypt, spent many years studying under Egyptian priests, and gained entrance to receive initiation in an Egyptian temple. He then visited Babylon to receive instruction from Zoroaster, known to the Babylonians as Zaratas and considered to be the wisest human being of that time. We learn that Pythagoras received initiation in Babylon from Zoroaster who, so it is said, cleansed him of the impurities of his previous life.

Through Zoroaster, Pythagoras learned of the mysteries of the cosmos and returned to Greece to begin to teach these mysteries in a new way, in a way different from the oriental manner of Zoroaster and the Babylonians, and different from the Egyptian priesthood.

Thus Pythagoras was a human being who received the rich treasures of the ancient mystery wisdom tradition, and brought them into Greek consciousness in a form appropriate for the Greeks, a form based on the principle of thinking. The mystery school that Pythagoras founded was at Croton in Southern Italy. We know very little about the content of the mysteries because Pythagoras' followers were sworn to secrecy, but it is clear that many cosmic mysteries were taught there.

Pythagoras is an important figure in the Sophia tradition, a bearer of the ancient wisdom, one who brought this wisdom into a new form, into a form that could be accepted, a form appropriate for human thinking consciousness. Later Greek philosophers such as Plato considered themselves as continuing on Pythagoras' path. Plato referred often to the teachings of the Pythagoreans and Plato's philosophy itself revolved around a central concept, that is, the world of ideas. For him the task of a philosopher was to gain access to the world of ideas. This teaching of Plato is actually none other than a pointing to Sophia as the wisdom of the cosmos. We could call Sophia, in the sense of Plato's philosophy, the "idea of ideas," the central wisdom from which all ideas have sprung. So Plato was in his own way devoted to the Divine Sophia.

As we can see, Sophia has been the shaping influence of major transitions in human culture and evolution. We recall that Sophia, as she herself indicates in the words with which she inspired King Solomon, was the handmaiden or co-worker of Yahweh in the Jewish tradition, as well as the inspiration of philosophy in Greece. It is important to keep this in mind and see how the history of philosophy unfolds after the period of Greek civilization.

Plato was a truly great philosopher, one who absorbed into himself the wisdom of the ages, the teachings of Sophia from the ancient mysteries, but who transformed it into a philosophical form. We might say that Plato's philosophy is really Sophianic mystery wisdom in idea form. If we look at the step from Plato to Aristotle we can see that another major transition took place. Aristotle was initially a pupil of Plato, but later developed his own philosophy and founded his own school in the city of Athens. Aristotle was concerned not so much with the world of ideas, but with the material world and the world of nature spread out around us. This was a dramatic shift. Aristotle in a certain respect was the founding philosopher of the Western scientific tradition. For Aristotle, what was important were the phenomena of nature—the clouds, the rivers, the fields, meteorology, astronomy, biology, ethics. These were the researches with which Aristotle occupied himself. So Aristotle, this extraordinary genius of the Western scientific tradition, gave the impulse for the turning away from the world of ideas to the natural world. This too was an important step, one that has led to the extraordinary achievements of Western civilization. These achievements would be unthinkable without the major stimulus provided by Aristotle.

Important for our considerations of the Sophia tradition are also the Stoic philosophers. They followed the philosophy of Heraclitus—an important figure in our considerations of the subsequent development of the Sophia tradition. Heraclitus lived in the city of Ephesus. He was an aristocrat, but decided at an early age he was going to dedicate his life to philosophy. Thus he renounced the privileges of his social rank, and entered into the precincts of the great temple of Artemis. He lived a hermit-like existence there and it was there he wrote his major work, *Periphysion*, meaning *About Physics* or *About Nature*. In this work, Heraclitus describes the Logos as the creative fire at the origin of all existence. This work for Heraclitus was a sacred task, and upon completion he brought it into the temple and laid it at the feet of the statue of Artemis. Unfortunately, we know next to nothing about the content of this work. What little we do know comes from commentaries by other people.

The Stoic philosophers were greatly influenced by Heraclitus and elaborated upon his view of the Logos as the creative fire, the creative power of existence.

Sophia and the Logos
One central consideration of the Sophia tradition involves the relationship between the Logos and Sophia. The entire Western cultural tradition was shaped essentially by the Logos, first in terms of philosophy inspired by the Logos, and then in terms of Christianity, which considers Christ as the incarnated Logos. The questions are: What happened to Sophia? And what is the relationship between Sophia and the Logos? Let us use an analogy to characterize this relationship. Logos means Word, and if we take Heraclitus' definition of the Logos as the creative fire present at the beginning of existence, it means that all creation came into existence through the Logos. Therefore, we can conceive of a divine Word that called all of existence into being. In order to form a conception of this we can consider the extraordinary power of sound. In the eighteenth century, the German physicist Ernst Chladni (1756–1827) demonstrated how sound vibrations form and shape particles of dust into

intricate shapes. We can conceive of the creative power of the Word as a form-shaping force in the whole of creation that calls forth all that we can see and experience around us in the material world. Preceding this material existence, therefore, was the creative power of the Word. This gives a picture of what Heraclitus is referring to as the creative fire of the Logos.

So where is Sophia in this picture, Sophia as divine wisdom? If we consider our own power of speech, it is to be hoped that intelligence or wisdom underlies what we say. Wisdom is, therefore, closely allied with the Word. Thus, in a broader context we can conceive of Sophia and the Logos working together in the creation—Sophia as Wisdom, the plan for the shaping of the creation, and the Logos as the power, the Word that informs and infuses the entire creation. Here we have an interweaving of Wisdom and the Word that we can conceive of as two halves of one reality. We can view the Logos as the masculine creative power of fire that shapes existence, and Sophia as Wisdom, the feminine shaping vessel or plan for the creation. In this way, we can form a picture of the relationship between the Logos and Sophia.

This is significant when we consider the development of philosophy in the West. In the philosophical tradition coming down through Pythagoras to Plato, the focus is more upon divine wisdom, Pythagoras having been a bridge between the ancient oriental mysteries and the new form of Sophia in early Greek culture. Whereas Plato may be seen as the philosopher who depicted the ancient wisdom in terms of the world of ideas, the central idea being Sophia. This we could call a feminine direction in philosophy.

On the other hand, looking at Heraclitus, the Stoics, and Aristotle, we see that the focus is on the masculine creative power of the Word, the Logos, and how this permeates creation. Platonic and

Aristotelian philosophy are contrasting—Plato's philosophy is Sophianic and Aristotle's philosophy is more related to the Logos. This is an important distinction, because the Aristotelian approach ultimately triumphed and has dominated the history of Western philosophy ever since. More importantly for our time, we find that this impulse toward the Logos is responsible for the emergence of Western science and technology.

I believe that science and technology have now reached a point of crisis and that a new direction has to emerge. There has been a one-sided masculine direction of development, and there needs to be a reorientation to the divine wisdom of Sophia, a turning toward what Plato calls the world of ideas. I think in the twentieth century we can see signs of this, for example in the psychology of C. G. Jung, who introduced the concept of archetypes. Archetypes are a new and modern form of expression of Plato's world of ideas.

Before tackling the problems of our modern culture we need to look at the causes for the gradual disappearance of Sophia in the West, and these can be discovered at the time of the founding of Christianity two thousand years ago. Later on we will explore in more detail how Sophia was lost or concealed. But for now, let us return to a consideration of the story of Perseus and Medusa in relation to our own time.

If we trace the development of Western thought up to the present, we can see that the great achievements of Western philosophy, theology, and science lead directly to the development of twentieth-century technology. Our world has been completely transformed through the application of science to technology. And yet we can also see an enormous threat and challenge to the whole future of the planet if this one-sided, Logocentric, rational mode of relationship continues to shape our world. This situation now amounts to a crisis, and it is calling us urgently in a new direction, one I believe that is to be given by Sophia through the opening-up of the qualities of the heart. With the advent of the computer, Western thought-life has come almost to a dead end, symbolically speaking, because the computer signifies a mechanization of human thought. It is not the living, creative thinking of a Plato or an Aristotle, but rather the mechanical thinking represented by the computer that we must guard against, if our thinking is to remain alive.

Of course, computers are extremely useful for all kinds of mechanical tasks involving calculation, tasks of banking, ordering, and so on. As long as the computer remains our servant there is nothing to be said against it. But the very real danger is that the servant is beginning to occupy our thinking more and more, and therefore is beginning to take over our thought life. This is an enormous danger, one that I see as a new and modern version of the Medusa myth. In other words, just as people of Medusa's time were turned to stone if they gazed directly upon her face, so in our time the computer screen becomes like the image of Medusa and could, so to say, turn us to stone if we sit motionless for endless hours in front of it. The warning here is that the evil eye of Medusa turned human beings to stone in the past, and it could happen again in our own time, not in a literal, but in a metaphorical sense. If we give up our own free, creative powers of thinking and substitute the mechanical thinking associated with the computer, we are in danger of losing our connection with divine wisdom. Further, by sitting for hours in front of the computer we risk losing our very ability to move, which is a God-given, creative faculty.

If we relived the great myth of Perseus and Medusa in our time, what would be the new challenge for Perseus? It would be the challenge to go beyond mechanical computer thinking with the help of divine wisdom, or Sophia. Just as three thousand years ago there was a transition from ancient clairvoyance to the rational thinking of Greek philosophy, so now there needs to take place a transition from mechanical thinking to a new kind of clairvoyance, a new seeing, a new thinking that is able to "see" in pictures. This is the transition that is to take place now. We can call this the thinking of the heart, and it is characterized by a new and radiant faculty of thought that is made possible through opening up the heart to the inspiration of Divine Sophia. This will develop our new faculty of seeing in a way that does not dampen down or blot out our thinking ability but which takes our thinking a stage further, to a place where thinking becomes a new way of seeing. This is the great transition that humanity is to make into the future. Before considering this new faculty, made possible by Divine Sophia, let us return to the question of how Sophia disappeared from Western culture and civilization.

Chapter Three
Why Sophia Disappeared
from Western Culture

W HY IS IT THAT SOPHIA DISAPPEARED AS THE source of inspiration from Western culture and civilization? This has to do with the relationship between Sophia and the Logos. Key to an understanding of this transition is the work of the Jewish philosopher Philo of Alexandria, a contemporary of Christ who died in about 45 CE. Philo was schooled in Greek thinking, and from the Stoics he adopted the conception of the Logos as the creative fire, or the power behind existence. Moreover, Philo had a notion of creation that included Sophia. As a Jew, he was of course familiar with the Wisdom Books of the Hebrew Scriptures attributed to Solomon, and so he had a living picture of Sophia as the wisdom of the creation. How did he incorporate these two, Sophia from the Hebrew tradition and the Logos from the Greek tradition, into his philosophy?

Philo depicts Yahweh as the Creator whose first act is the creation of Sophia. Then he conceives Yahweh, through Sophia or together with Sophia, creating the cosmos, which he identifies as the Son of Yahweh and Sophia. He identifies the cosmos, the creation, with the Logos. In Philo's philosophy, Yahweh is the creator, Sophia is the wisdom of the creation, and their Son is the Logos, the created cosmos. In Philo's description, there is the notion that Sophia's divine wisdom was imparted to the Son, the Logos.

In reading the philosophy of Philo of Alexandria it becomes quite difficult to distinguish between Sophia and the Logos. This is a key factor in the disappearance of Sophia in later Western civilization. Philo's ideas provided a powerful stimulus for commentary by many of the Church fathers, for some of whom Sophia actually became identified with the Logos because of this similarity in the description. Thus, Origen of Alexandria, one of the great Greek Church fathers, describes Sophia as being identical with the Logos. Other theologians among the Church fathers point to Sophia as being identical with the Holy Spirit. The main thrust, however, came with the identification of Sophia with the Logos. Let us look into this in more detail.

The Arian Controversy
In the early history of Christianity the clash about the identity of Sophia came to be known as the Arian controversy. Arius was Bishop of Alexandria and he held to the notion that the Logos is a created being. For him, as with Origen, Sophia and the Logos were the same being. Crucial to an understanding of this are the words found at the beginning of the Gospel of St. John:

In the beginning was the Word, and the Word was with God and the Word was God. This was in the beginning with God. All

things were made through the Word, and nothing that was made
was made without the Word.

We might rephrase this statement as follows: *In the beginning was the*
Logos, and all things were made through the Logos, and nothing that was
made was made without the Logos. John's formulation confirms that he
was familiar with concepts of Greek philosophy, in particular with the
concept of the Logos. It is possible that he received this idea through
Philo of Alexandria. However, as John wrote his Gospel in Ephesus,
it is also possible that, ultimately, Heraclitus of Ephesus was the
source of John's knowledge of the Logos. If we take the statement of
John, that *the Logos was in the beginning and that all things were made*
through the Logos, and compare this with Sophia's statement in the
Book of Proverbs, *I was created at the beginning of the works of the*
Lord, then we can see that if one were to identify the Logos and
Sophia, one could come to the conclusion, as Arius did, that the
Logos is a created being. This view was fiercely opposed by
Athanasius, another early Christian theologian of the fourth century,
and this clash of philosophical positions became known as the great
Arian controversy.

Athanasius held to the conviction that the Logos is not a created
being, but is of the same substance as the Creator, so that the Father
and the Son are inwardly connected. As he wrote: *The Father begets*
the Son but does not create the Son. The Son is of one and the same
substance as the Father. Athanasius fiercely opposed Arius' teaching
that the Son was created by the Father. Arius stated: *The Son was*
created and established by the Father before the eons. He is not eternal or
uncreated like the Father, and also does not have the same manner of
being as the Father.

41

Interestingly, Athanasius agreed with the identification of the Logos and Sophia, but arrived at a different interpretation:

> *We have rebelled against the unreasonable and delusional conceptions of Arius. It is simply not right to call the Son a creature. We have also learned to read the passage in Proverbs correctly. It is written there, "The Lord created me, the first of his works, long ago."*
>
> *The meaning that is hidden here, and the right interpretation, has to be sought. This passage cannot simply be understood as if the meaning were openly revealed. If what is written here were to refer to an angel or to some other existing being, the expression "He created me" could be used as it could with one of us creatures. If, however, it is God's Sophia, in whom all existing things have been created, who speaks thusly of herself, one can only think that she wants to say by the words "He created" nothing other than "He begot." Wisdom does not speak of herself saying "I am a creature" but only "the Lord created me, the first of his works, long ago." The expression "He created" does not mean that what is referred to as created is necessarily or according to its substance a creature.*

Here Athanasius tries to defend his view that the Logos is not a created being, by taking the identification of the Logos with Sophia and trying to reinterpret Sophia's own statement in Proverbs that she was created at the beginning of time.

The Arian controversy dominated the first Ecumenical Council called by Emperor Constantine the Great in 325 CE. The Church fathers ultimately condemned the ideas of Arius, while those of

Athanasius triumphed and became the central teachings of Christianity. In this process, however, we find that Sophia became identified with the Logos and was pushed into the background, indeed was more or less forgotten. So, although early Christianity inherited the Old Testament Books of Wisdom relating to Divine Sophia, because of the identification of Sophia with the Logos, Sophia was omitted from the history of Western Christianity, and, while she was not completely lost, she receded into the background.

Looking back over the course of Western civilization we can begin to grasp the magnitude of the tragedy caused by this identification. It meant that a feeling for the Divine Feminine and relationship to the Divine Sophia was lost in Christianity. As a result, the whole evolution of Christianity has been in the spirit of a one-sided rational development that parallels the development of modern science and technology. The feminine mode of thought, the thinking of the heart, became more and more excluded from Christian thinking, and now this imbalance needs to be corrected.

One example of this tragic loss of Sophia from Christianity is that Christianity has by and large ignored the world of nature. For the Greeks, nature *was* Mother Earth, or Demeter, and when she was forgotten the ancient mystery centers dedicated to the Divine Feminine—Artemis in Ephesus, Demeter at Eleusis, and the mysteries connected with Isis in Egypt—that were described in the last chapter were closed down one by one. We see here evidence of an evolutionary tendency to exclude the Divine Feminine around the time of Christ two thousand years ago. The reason for this we find in Christianity itself; namely, that with the coming of Christ the Divine Masculine was to be placed in the foreground. Here I am referring to Christ's teaching where he speaks of himself and the Father as being one. He also uses the expression, *No-one comes to the Father but by me*, and he teaches the *Lord's Prayer*, the central prayer of Christianity, which starts with the words, *Our Father*.

If we look at the emergence of Christianity, we see that Christ came into a patriarchal society, into the world of Israel, and that he chose male disciples. Christ's teaching took place in the context of this patriarchal culture. If Christ had incarnated as a woman, his message would have been rejected by the patriarchal culture of Israel. It was inevitable that Christ came into a male body, and affirmed his relationship to the divine Father. In a certain respect we can understand this emphasis on the Divine Masculine that took place with the coming of Christ two thousand years ago. It was part of the development that we find prefigured in Greek philosophy with the transition from Plato to Aristotle. We saw that whereas Plato directed us to the world of ideas, to the Divine Sophia, Aristotle focussed on the rational aspects of the Logos. Aristotelian philosophy triumphed, we might say, over Platonic philosophy. And, in this way, Aristotle was preparing for the coming incarnation of the Logos as Christ. Moreover, Aristotelian philosophy provided a strong bedrock for the later development of Christianity. St. Thomas Aquinas, who is viewed as the greatest Christian theologian, built his whole philosophy upon that of Aristotle. Here we see the Logos being emphasized to the exclusion of Sophia.

Why did this transition take place? One reason is that the over-emphasis upon the Logos, the masculine side of existence, had to take place in order for Western humanity to develop its philosophical, theological, and scientific faculties. Western civilization would be unthinkable without this one-sided development. We recall that the mythological world of the Greeks in antiquity gave way to a conception of the one divine being, the Logos, Christ, who incarnated upon the Earth for the Earth's transformation and redemption. The activation of human will and intelligence to participate in this work of redemption took place at the expense of the more feminine qualities of the heart.

On the other hand, if we look at the actual teachings of Christ, we find that he himself also embodied these feminine qualities. He was surrounded not just by male disciples but by holy women—his mother the Virgin Mary, Mary Magdalene, her sister Martha, and other holy women. These women provide an important clue to Christ's deeper message, which was in a more profound sense about the balancing or marriage of the masculine and the feminine. However, the context of his teaching necessitated bringing forth the masculine side, causing the Sophianic side of existence to fade into the background.

Here and there, however, we find this Sophianic side does manifest. A couple of passages in the New Testament attest to this. For example, in his letter to the Ephesians, St. Paul refers to divine wisdom when he says:

> *To me, who am less than the least of all God's people, he has granted the privilege of proclaiming to the Gentiles the good news of the unfathomable riches of Christ and the bringing to light how this hidden purpose was to be put into effect. It lay concealed for long ages with God, the creator of the universe, in order that now through the church the wisdom of God in its infinite variety might be made known to the rulers and authorities in the heavenly realms. This accords with his age-long purpose, which he accomplished in Christ Jesus our Lord.*

This text proclaims a personal experience of Sophia. It refers to the unfathomable mystery of divine wisdom kept secret by the Creator but which through Christ was revealed. However, the most significant reference to Sophia is found in Chapter Twelve of the Book of Revelation. Here, John speaks of a great sign appearing in the heavens of a woman clothed by the Sun, with the Moon under her feet, and on her head a crown of twelve stars. This is a dramatic image of Divine Sophia as the wisdom of the cosmos who embraces all the stars and planets, the Sun and the Moon, and who shines from the cosmos as the World Soul. We find this idea taken up by the neo-Platonists who spoke of Sophia as the World Soul or the soul of the cosmos. This is a true definition of Divine Sophia.

Our examples show that there are references, even within Christianity, to Sophia, but that these are few and far between. Generally speaking, they were gradually lost from the main current of Christianity. On the other hand, outside of Christianity—I have referred already to the Neo-Platonists—there was still a conception of Sophia as a living being, where the ideas of Sophia broke through. In the later tradition, we find that they occurred in a more or less mystical context.

The Virgin Mary and the Female Followers of Jesus

It is quite clear that the incarnation of the Logos as Christ was the stimulus for a major transition in human evolution; but this transition was also brought about by Divine Sophia. Part of the mystery of Christ's incarnation as the Logos presupposes the incarnation of Sophia as a parallel event, but one that signified the holding-back of Sophia in order to allow the Logos to come into the foreground. If we look at the actual events taking place around the

Christ, we find that Sophia is truly represented on the one hand in the figure of the Virgin Mary, and on the other hand by Mary Magdalene and her sister Martha who were close companions of Jesus. If we wish to grasp the deeper significance of the Sophianic element surrounding and accompanying the life of Christ, we must look at the special relationship between Jesus and these holy women. Primarily, we must focus on the Virgin Mary, his mother, who embodied the qualities of the divine wisdom of Sophia. She was a being of extraordinary purity whose heart was fully open, who could read the thoughts of those around her, and who was the life and soul of the community of disciples gathered together by Jesus Christ. Mary was open on the one hand to the people around her, in silent knowledge of what was taking place within them, and on the other hand she was open to the cosmos and also to the Earth. The Virgin Mary embodies the qualities of a heartfelt awareness of our fellow human beings, a sense of connectedness with the whole cosmos, and of unity with the Earth. In this respect the Virgin Mary was a forerunner, a model for future humanity, for she embodies the very qualities we need to develop in the future.

We find that different attributes of the Divine Feminine are represented by the other women close to Jesus. Mary Magdalene and Martha were the sisters of Lazarus, a wealthy man who lived in Bethany, which was close to Jerusalem. There are great mysteries connected with the fact that Lazarus, Mary Magdalene, and Martha each related to a different aspect of Christ's being. As is also the case with the Virgin Mary, we might describe Lazarus as the spiritual companion of Jesus. It was he who was raised from the dead by Christ in order to fulfill a great mission. Mary Magdalene might be seen as the soul companion of Jesus, for she was the human being who beheld him at the time of the resurrection on Easter Sunday morning. When she entered the garden containing the Holy Sepulchre, Mary Magdalene beheld someone. She first thought he was the gardener and then realized that this was her Master who had risen from the dead. The appearance of the risen Christ to Mary Magdalene after the crucifixion indicates something of the profound relationship between them. Thirdly, Martha was the one who attended to the physical needs of Jesus and the community of disciples. She was active in helping them, in caring for them, and making sure the necessities of life were available. Here again we can see aspects of the Divine Sophia shining through with the Virgin Mary as a complete embodiment of Divine Sophia on a spiritual level, with Mary Magdalene on the soul level, and with Martha on the bodily level.

It is a central element of the Sophia teachings to grasp these three aspects of Divine Sophia as they relate to humanity. Jesus Christ, the incarnated Logos, points to the Father, but through his relationship to the holy women around him he is bringing to expression the relationship of the Logos to Sophia, the Divine Feminine. In his teaching and deeds it is implicitly shown that there is an intimate interweaving taking place all the time between the Logos and Wisdom, between Christ and Sophia.

One example of this is the first miracle performed by Jesus, described in the Gospel of St. John, where he changed the water into wine for the wedding of Nathanael of Cana and his bride. Jesus and his mother and many of the disciples had been invited to the wedding in the little town of Cana, northeast of Nazareth, and, as described in the Gospel of St. John, Jesus had the responsibility for providing the second course of wine after the celebratory meal. John describes how, after the first course of wine, Mary reminded Jesus that he was responsible for the second course of wine. Mary's reminder to Jesus reveals something of the guiding quality of Sophia, through Mary addressing the Logos in Jesus. Jesus then gave the command that six vessels of water were to be fetched and, after blessing the water, he performed the miracle of turning the water into wine. The water symbolizes the water of life being transformed into wine through the power of divine love represented by the Logos. Christ brought down the fire of divine love into the water of wisdom, and in this magical act we can see the mystery of the interweaving between the Logos and Sophia. All those who drank of this wine were filled with the power of divine love and were united in the community in which they recognized Christ as the Chosen One.

We can also interpret this miracle in the following way. The entire history of the people of Israel was through its kings and prophets guided by Divine Sophia, and this guidance can be likened to a stream of living water flowing down through the ages. The incarnation of the Logos as the power of divine love comes into this stream of wisdom and transforms it into wine. The miracle of turning the water into wine is thus a symbol of the cosmic interweaving of wisdom, Sophia, and the Logos, Christ.

The entire life of Jesus is an expression of this interweaving of divine love and divine wisdom. And although Sophia, or the Divine Feminine, faded into the background of Western culture, she nevertheless plays an integral part in the plan of evolution. The aspect of divine love borne by the Logos moved into the foreground, and has been the inspiration for Western humanity down through the ages and into our present time. Now, however, I would like to reiterate, for it is fundamental to our time, we are entering a New Age in which the impulse of Divine Sophia, having been held back over the last two thousand years, is to come into the foreground again. The challenge of our time is to welcome Divine Sophia into our lives, and to let divine wisdom begin to speak to us again. We need to allow this wisdom, which has been held back for so long, to become the inspiring, guiding voice in human hearts now and in the future.

We have considered the inspiration and guiding power of Divine Sophia in human affairs as far back as King Solomon in antiquity, and in the Greek and Egyptian mysteries. Throughout the ages she has been ever-present, inspiring different religions and spiritual traditions as the ageless or perennial wisdom. Then we saw how Sophia revealed herself in the founding of Christianity, but held herself back in order to allow the voice of the Logos to sound in full strength through the mystery of its incarnation in Christ. In tracing her influence we come to the conclusion that Sophia's work in antiquity was largely to prepare the way for the great event of Christ's incarnation. St. Augustine confirms this when says of Plato that he was a "Christian" in pre-Christian times, one who was preparing the way for the incarnation of the Logos. Even in Buddhism we can see a preparation for this event, because Buddha brought the teaching of living out of compassion, and Christ is the one who actually embodied the divine power of love and compassion to which Buddha was referring.

In the overarching plan of evolution we can see that Divine Sophia was ever present, preparing the way with different groups of human beings in different parts of the Earth that would eventually all come together in the central event of Christ's incarnation. We recall that at that momentous time, Sophia held herself back. What does this really signify? If we liken it to how a mother loves, cares for, and educates her child, we realize that when her child comes of age the mother must stand back and allow the child to stand alone, to become free and independent. The incarnation of Christ signifies that the particular moment of evolution had been reached which truly represented the coming age of humanity. Thus, for the past two thousand years, freedom, independence, and creativity of thinking have been the hallmarks of Western culture. They have been the heady source of breathtaking scientific and technological advances. However, due to the imbalance this one-sided rational development has caused, it is now time for Divine Sophia to speak once again.

The cosmological aspects of the Sophia teachings reveal that with the twenty-first century we have the beginning of the inpouring of the Divine Feminine as the world-transforming power of the future. We are at the threshold of the coming of age of humanity. What does this age signify? It signifies the birth of our true identity, our true ego in the sense of a divine ego. And, not surprisingly, this coming of age was clearly prefigured in the incarnation of Christ as the Logos. In the context of the Sophia teachings, Christ is the divine Self, the divine I AM, who came to the world to be born into each human being. We find this conveyed in the words of St. Paul: *Not I, but Christ in me.* All the mysteries connected with the life of Christ have to do with this turning point in time and the coming of age of humanity.

During the life of Jesus, Sophia was present and manifesting subtly through the Virgin Mary and the holy women around him, but she held back in order that the divine I AM could be the primary influence upon humanity for the next two thousand years. In fact, Christ's incarnation signified the beginning of a new astrological cycle; it was toward the end of the Age of Aries, approaching the start of the Age of Pisces. We will focus on this in more detail in Chapter Nine. For now, we can say that Sophia held back at that moment in time waiting for the emergence of the divine self of humanity to become active, so that each human being could begin to find him- or herself as a divine being, free and independent. But just as every mother, in releasing her offspring into the world at their coming of age, longs for and treasures the time when her offspring will return to find a new relationship with her on a higher level, so it is Sophia's hope, as the mother of humanity, that her "children" will find a new relationship to her and will enter into connection with her being in a new and creative way. This is the threshold in time that we have reached now at the beginning of the twenty-first century, when a new inflowing of the Divine Feminine is taking place. Divine Sophia can speak to us again in a new way but on a higher level than in antiquity when she was, in her ageless wisdom, the comforter and caring mother of humanity. In our modern times her guiding influence will redress the imbalance caused by the one-sided rational and scientific development, and offer the possibility of bringing the Divine Masculine and Divine Feminine into balance within each human being. The great promise of our time is that, with our cooperation, Divine Sophia will be the guiding power and inspiration for the next major transition in humanity's evolution.

Chapter Four
The Influence of Divine Sophia
in the Western Mystical Tradition

L ET US LOOK NOW AT THE COURSE OF THE SOPHIA
teachings in the historical period following the incarnation of
Christ, when, as has been stated, the Logos moved into the
foreground and influenced the central teachings of Christianity. In
the twentieth century there began a new inflowing of the divine
wisdom associated with Sophia. However, in the 2000 years since the
birth of Christ, manifestations and actual revelations of Divine
Sophia have occurred here and there, generally speaking in a hidden
way. In other words, there were certain individuals who experienced
Sophia as the mother of humanity in the period after the birth of
Christ and before the New Age beginning in the twentieth century.
So we can speak of a Sophia tradition, albeit a hidden one. Let us
bring forward the names of significant individuals who contributed
to this Sophia tradition.

St. Augustine plays an important role because among the Church
fathers he was the one most occupied with Sophia. St. Augustine was

born in 354 CE in Africa and died in the year 430 CE. In his writings he distinguishes between two Sophias, one of whom is the uncreated wisdom, the uncreated Sophia, whom St. Augustine considers to be the Logos, the Christ, the begotten Son of the Father. The other is the created Sophia, divine wisdom, who was created at the beginning of the Creation. Let me highlight one passage from St. Augustine, where he speaks of created Sophia in an individual and personal way:

This Sophia is from you, O God, but something quite different from you. Although we do not find temporality in her, nevertheless she is able to change, whereby she could turn away from God. But she does not do that. For she is bound to God with a great love.

Although she is not equally eternal to you, she is not constrained by transitions in time, and experiences no difference of time and is not extended in time, but instead rests in eternal contemplation of your being.

Elsewhere St. Augustine refers to created Sophia as: *Our mother Jerusalem who is above and free, eternal in heaven.* He also says that she is the pure and most harmoniously single mind: *The place of peace of blessed spirits in heaven and above the heavens.* St. Augustine held that the uncreated Sophia is the illuminating light of existence, and that the created Sophia is the illuminated light. St. Augustine's distinction is one that has influenced many subsequent theologians and prominent figures in Christian history.

In the Middle Ages, we find a remarkable and extraordinary revelation of Sophia through St. Hildegard of Bingen, who was born in 1098 and died at the age of eighty-one in 1179. Associated with Bingen near the Rhine, in Germany, Hildegard was from early childhood aware of being surrounded by divine light and was able to see beyond the natural world into heavenly realms of existence. She became a nun, and later assumed the post of head of her monastery. Although she was of weak physical constitution, this did not deter her from travelling around to meet her contemporaries and having correspondence with many significant individuals of her time. She had contact with popes and kings, and had profound influence in the areas of religion, science, and medicine of the twelfth century. In fact, today there is something of a renaissance of interest in Hildegard of Bingen, and as a result numerous books are currently available about her work. These include her thoughts about medicine, her references to the therapeutic properties of precious stones, and recordings of music she composed.

Among St. Hildegard's most powerful and inspiring visions were those of the Divine Sophia, which have been published in more recent times. For Hildegard, Sophia was on the one hand the mother and soul of the world, and on the other hand she saw Sophia as the bride of Christ and the mother of the Church. Sometimes she combined both aspects. Hildegard says this of Sophia in the *Book of Divine Works:*

And I saw within the mystery of God a wondrously beautiful image. It had a human form and its countenance was of such beauty and radiance that I could have more easily gazed at the sun.

Accompanying her vision, St. Hildegard heard a voice saying: *With Sophia I have rightly put the universe in order.* The voice continued:

For what you see in God's mystery as a marvelously beautiful figure similar to a human being signifies the love of our heavenly Father. On this account the countenance is of such beauty and splendor that you can more easily gaze at the sun than at it.

In another of her visions St. Hildegard says:

God has established the firmament in wisdom and secured it by power of the stars. Both sun and moon are an adornment of wisdom. The firmament is the throne of all beauty. God furnished all this beauty for the divine glory as it was pre-ordained in wisdom. Creation was Sophia's garment because Sophia clothes her own achievement in the same way as we human beings wear clothes. All of Sophia's decrees are gentle and mild. Since she washes her garments, whenever they become sullied, in the blood of the merciful Lamb. Therefore Sophia should be loved more than all the beauty of creation. She is known to be worthy of love by all the saints because they can never become weary of gazing at her dear form.

Sophia in the Middle Ages and Beyond

Very often the question is raised whether Sophia is an attribute of God as Divine Wisdom, or whether she is an actual person. Some think that the words of Sophia in the Books of Wisdom from the Old Testament show her to be Lady Wisdom, a personification of God's wisdom, who addresses humanity. However, if we study the actual words and indications of Sophia in the Wisdom Books of the Old Testament, I think it emerges quite clearly that Sophia is a *being*. We can summarize the Wisdom Books as leading to an understanding of

Sophia as a *person* in that in the Holy Scripture she is proclaimed as a spiritual nature with the qualities, attributes, and functions of a person, such as having reason and free will. Furthermore, she is described as being created female. She is different from God and acts independently with respect to God. For example, she is described as dancing before God. She advises God and she actively participates in the work of creation with God. With respect to the creation she is depicted as guiding, renewing, and ruling everywhere with reason, power, and goodness. With respect to humanity, she is described as admonishing, leading, and assisting us as mother, teacher, and beloved. Moreover, the Christian tradition, from the Church fathers to the present, has often understood Sophia as a person, even if interpretations about her have varied.

As we recall, some theologians identified her with the Logos and others identified her with the Holy Spirit. However, the testimonies of mystics such as Hildegard of Bingen and Jakob Boehme make it quite clear that they had a direct, living experience of Sophia as a being, as a person. Their testimony bears witness to Sophia as a person and not simply as a personification of divine wisdom.

In addition to the testimonies of mystics such as Hildegard of Bingen and Jakob Boehme, there are many depictions of Sophia as an actual being in the art of the Middle Ages. For example in Herrad von Landsberg's work, *The Garden of Delights*, from around the twelfth century, Sophia is depicted as queen of the seven liberal arts— grammar, rhetoric, dialectic, music, arithmetic, geometry, and astronomy. Here we see Sophia sitting on a royal throne in the center, surrounded by the seven liberal arts. A stream of water pours from each side of her body. Below her are the philosophers Plato and Aristotle, the recipients of the living water of Sophia's wisdom. The seven liberal arts are depicted as women positioned around Sophia's inner circle. In such works we see that artists also had their experience of Divine Sophia, and the depiction of Sophia as the patron or queen of the seven liberal arts is something very significant. We will return to this theme later.

Let us now focus upon Jakob Boehme's visions and experiences of Sophia, for here again we find a powerful and extraordinary testimony to Sophia as a divine being existing in spiritual realms, with whom we can have communication and a relationship. Jakob Boehme was born in 1575 the son of a poor farmer living in a little village near Gorlitz in the region of Germany then known as Schlesia. He was brought up in the Lutheran faith at a time when Protestant theology was dominant. However, this proved to be difficult for him on account of his mystical inclinations. Even as a youth, Jakob Boehme was deeply religious. He learned the cobbler's trade and became a journeyman apprentice, which was customary at the time. The experience of injustice and evil weighed heavily on his sensitive nature and stood in the background of the mystical experiences that began during this period of his life. During his first mystical experience, young Jakob felt himself bathed in a supernatural light and a blessed sense of peace that lasted for seven days.

Boehme returned home around 1594, opened a cobbler's shop, and shortly thereafter married a woman from Gorlitz who bore him four sons. Around 1600 he had a second mystical experience while watching the splendid glow of sunlight on a pewter jug. It seemed to Boehme that he became aware of forces active within the jug that gave him insight into the foundation of things, and into questions which had troubled him for some time. After this second experience, Boehme had a number of visions and realizations that further deepened his insight. He remained silent about these visions until a third experience around 1610 seemed to unify everything. At this point he began to record his experiences and visions, and this resulted in his first work, *Aurora*, which can be translated as *Rising Dawn*.

Although a source of enormous consolation and blessing, Jakob Boehme's visions and mystical experiences also brought him much grief and suffering. He was attacked from the pulpit by the Lutheran pastor of Gorlitz, who branded him as a heretic, and he was forbidden to write of his experiences. Boehme honored this prohibition for some years, but, in 1619, urged on by his friends and by his own inner voice, he began to record his visions once again. He continued composing works until the end of his life.

One of Jakob Boehme's most significant visions was that of an appearance of the Divine Sophia. Boehme writes:

I rely upon her faithful promise when she appeared to me that she wanted to change all my sorrow into great joy. As I was prostrate upon the mountain around midnight and many kinds of storms engulfed me, she came to comfort me and wedded herself to me.

This particular mystical experience took place when Boehme was under personal attack during his years of silence. Boehme indicates that his knowledge of Sophia increased after this vision, and he ascribes to her seven qualities or characteristics— keen, soft, firm, serious, clear, pure, and persuasive. For Boehme, Sophia is the exhalation or out-breath of God's power. She is God's mirror and the image of God's goodness. She dwells in pious souls, and is the friend, betrothed, bride, mistress, and teacher to those who seek her in the appropriate manner. She gives immortality to those who unite themselves with her. She is the source of joy and pure desire and is sent by God to mediate between God and humanity and to help and comfort all. For Boehme, Sophia is truly his spiritual friend and bride, mother and teacher.

Due to his inspiring visions that testify to the Divine Sophia, Jakob Boehme has become known as the father of Sophiology in the West—Sophiology being the science of Sophia. Throughout his writings, Boehme refers to Sophia as the true friend, the one who is able to enter into conversation with his soul. In another passage he writes:

The figure of God's wisdom, Sophia, is that of a decorous virgin in the likeness of the Trinity, an image similar to that of the angels and human beings, like a flower growing out of God's Spirit. For she is a being of the Spirit, like a garment with which He reveals Himself, otherwise His form would not be known. In this eternal mirror of the wisdom of God (Sophia) is also beheld the soul of humanity in its essence, which with the beginning of the first movement in God was formed into creatures. Sophia is the mother of all creatures, the matrix in which are heaven, the stars, the elements, the Earth, and everything that lives and grows, contained as if in a single image.

As with Hildegard of Bingen, we see that Jakob Boehme was blessed with the grace of a revelation of Divine Sophia; he was someone who allowed his heart and mind to open to Sophia and to receive her instruction. His works bear witness to the tremendous inspiration and presence of Divine Sophia, and they powerfully convey this quality of inspiration to others. In fact Boehme's writings served as a seed impulse that had great influence not only upon the German cultural tradition, but that crossed over to England, and even extended all the way to Russia. In fact, understanding the unfolding of the Sophia tradition in our time would be impossible without taking into account the great contribution of Jakob Boehme.

One key element in Boehme's teaching of Sophia concerns the profound relationship existing between Sophia and the Virgin Mary. Boehme was perhaps the first to have the intuition of an incorporation, or perhaps even incarnation, of the Divine Sophia in Mary. He declared:

> *Sophia was above all chosen, and sent to unite with Mary and to strengthen her, so that she was capable of becoming the mother of the incarnating Logos. Mary, an ornament to the most blessed heavenly virgin, [was] the earthly virgin who attracted the beautiful heavenly virgin Sophia.*

The relationship between Sophia and the Virgin Mary is something that became of central importance for the Russian Sophiologists, although it's unclear whether or not they adopted this idea from Boehme. His testimony has nonetheless inspired numerous individuals since that time to turn to Divine Sophia, including John Pordage and Jane Leade in England. In Germany we find that Gottfried Arnold, the poet Novalis, and the great Idealist philosopher Friedrich Wilhelm Joseph von Schelling (1775–1854) were all inspired through reading the works of Jakob Boehme. Lastly, Vladimir Solovyev, the great Russian philosopher and founder of Sophiology in Russia, was also inspired and influenced by Jakob

Boehme. Thus we can see that Boehme is a central and key figure, a shining beacon in the Sophia tradition.

Anne Catherine Emmerich

One of the most gifted clairvoyants of all time was Anne Catherine Emmerich, who bears witness in her works to Divine Sophia and her relationship with the Virgin Mary. Anne Catherine Emmerich was born in 1774 and died in 1824. She was a contemporary of Goethe and Beethoven at a time of an extraordinary flourishing of German culture. She is a great source of inspiration to me personally because her visions convey in a remarkably pure way the essence of the life and work of Christ and Mary.

At an early age, Anne Catherine Emmerich joined the Augustinian order. Later, at the age of thirty-eight, she received the stigmata. From this time onward she was confined to her bed in extraordinary suffering. She ate hardly anything, existing on the Host and water, but she received a continual stream of visions concerning the lives of Christ and Mary. Because she had received the stigmata, many spiritual seekers from all over Germany visited her. Among them was Clemens Brentano, the German Romantic poet, who was so deeply impressed by what he experienced in her presence that he decided to give up what he was doing and move from Berlin to be near her and record her visions. Emmerich had a vision confirming the coming of one whom she described as the pilgrim. When Clemens Brentano arrived, she recognized him as the one from her vision, and he indeed remained with her, as had been prophesied, and wrote down her visions.

During this work together, Anne Catherine Emmerich began to receive visions day by day describing the life of Christ. I have been able to show that Anne Catherine Emmerich's visions are by and large authentic and they provided the basis for my research into determining the chronology of the life of Christ. Her visions enabled me to determine the date of his birth, his baptism in the Jordan, the feeding of the five thousand, and many other events. All of this research enables us to have a new understanding of the Gospels and of the work of Jesus Christ set in temporal and geographical context. From this standpoint alone it is clear that Anne Catherine Emmerich's visions constitute a remarkable gift to humanity, and it is thanks to Clemens Brentano that we have them in written form.

To highlight the remarkable power of Anne Catherine Emmerich's clairvoyance I must mention the historic discovery of the Virgin Mary's house near Ephesus in Turkey. This discovery, that took place in 1891, was made solely on the basis of Anne Catherine Emmerich's visions describing its location. Two Lazarite priests, who had read the account in her vision, decided that they would conduct a search for the house of the Virgin Mary in Ephesus. On account of the precise description furnished by Anne Catherine Emmerich, they were able to trace the exact location of this house. Archeological investigations show that the remains of the house they discovered date back to the first century. The house has been reconstructed according to the visions received by Anne Catherine Emmerich, and it is now a center of pilgrimage visited by people from all over the world. Anyone who visits Ephesus, as I did in 1996, can experience the truly blessed quality in surrounding nature, and the extraordinary outpouring of love that greets one when entering this little house, in which, according to Anne Catherine Emmerich, the death of the Virgin Mary and her ascension into heaven took place. It is a place where one feels that the heavens are open, where a divine feminine presence streams in as a power of blessing. Also in the vicinity, a wonderful spring of holy water issues forth.

Anne Catherine Emmerich's visions provide the most extensive description of the Virgin Mary that has ever been revealed to humanity. From this we can also gain a feeling for Divine Sophia as a pre-existent being who, at a certain moment in time, entered into the soul of the Virgin Mary. A few passages from the visions of Anne Catherine Emmerich highlight this description of the pre-existence of Sophia in relation to the Virgin Mary.

The first passage refers to an event involving the prophet Elijah on Mount Carmel. There had been a drought in Israel for three and a half years and Elijah, on Mount Carmel, prayed that it might rain. Eventually a little cloud appeared above the Mediterranean. These are the words of Anne Catherine Emmerich:

> *In this little cloud I saw from the first a little shining figure like a virgin. The head of this virgin was encircled with rays. She stretched her arms out in the form of a cross and had a triumphal wreath hanging from one hand. She appeared as if hovering above the whole Promised Land in the cloud as it spread even further.*
>
> *I saw how this cloud divided into different parts and fell in eddying showers of crystal dew on certain holy and consecrated places inhabited by devout men and by those who were praying for salvation. I saw these showers edged with the colors of the rainbow and the blessing take shape in their midst, like a pearl in its shell.*

In this vision we have an image of Sophia as the bestower of blessings upon those who turn toward her, and at the same time it is a presentiment of the incarnation of the Virgin Mary. Another vision concerns the incarnation of the Virgin Mary:

> *I had a vision of the creation of Mary's most holy soul and of its being united with her most pure body. In the glory by which the most holy Trinity is usually represented in my visions I saw a movement, like a great shining mountain, and yet also like a human figure. I saw something rise out of the midst of this figure towards its mouth and go forth from it like a shining brightness. Then I saw this brightness standing separate before the face of God, turning and shaping itself, or rather being shaped. For I saw that while this brightness took human form, yet it was by the will of God that it received a form so unspeakably beautiful. I saw too that God showed the beauty of this soul to the angels and that they had unspeakable joy in its beauty.*

Emmerich then describes the descent of this beautiful soul into the womb of St. Anne, the mother of the Virgin Mary:

> *In this same instant I saw Our Lady's holy mother raise herself on her couch surrounded by light. She was in ecstasy, and had a vision of her womb opening like a tabernacle to enclose a shining little virgin from whom mankind's salvation was to spring.*

In the visions of Anne Catherine Emmerich we have also a testimony to Sophia as the wisdom of God, as a being who incarnated into the Virgin Mary, and also bestowed blessings upon the holy men and women of Israel.

A few years after the death of Anne Catherine Emmerich, the Russian philosopher Vladimir Solovyev emerged as the great prophet of the Sophia tradition in Russia. Solovyev, who was born in 1853 and died in 1900, accomplished much in his short life in bringing Sophianic philosophy to the Russian people. With Solovyev we find a human being whose thinking is heart-inspired, imbued with a warmth of humanity, a clarity of light, and an intensity of purpose and direction that makes him one of the most outstanding philosophers of the modern age.

Divine Sophia is the central idea in Solovyev's philosophy. On Ascension Day in 1862 Solovyev had a profound vision of the Divine Sophia. He was only nine years old. While attending the liturgy in the university chapel in Moscow, the heavens suddenly opened and a majestic feminine figure wrapped in azure blue appeared to young Vladimir. This mystical experience was a powerful incentive for the young man to pursue a path of spiritual study that led him many years later to study in the library of the British Museum in London. It was here that he immersed himself in many religious and spiritual works, among them the writings of Jakob Boehme, in his quest to understand the vision of the Sophia he had had at the age of nine.

One day, while studying in the British Museum, Solovyev had a second vision of Divine Sophia, in which the face of Sophia appeared to him and he heard the words, "Go to Egypt." He followed the instruction from Sophia, made preparations, travelled to Egypt, and put up in a hotel in Cairo. It was here in Egypt that he had his third and greatest vision of Divine Sophia.

Solovyev describes his three mystical experiences of Sophia in a poem he wrote towards the end of his life. Referring to the appearance of Sophia to him in the library at the British Museum, Solovyev wrote:

I said to her, "Yes I saw you, but only your countenance heavenly radiant. O eternal Friend, hear my plea, and reveal all of yourself, as once to the child, to me!" "On to Egypt!" echoed within me.

Was it recklessness to act? No matter. Listening, without doubting, soon I was in a train for Paris, Lyons, Turin, Ancona, Bari. Everything flew past, mattering little. Soon I embarked from Brindisi through the waves bound on a British steamer to the land of the Nile. In Cairo I found welcome. Russians were there a-plenty, from Moscow too, from the city of my birth. Watching all the while for her sign.

And lo, in night's stillness, she gently wafted through my room.

"On to the desert! I await you!"

Thus day found me wandering towards the desert, unconcerned about provision. The sun was sinking and duskless darkness followed. Black was the star-twinkling night. All was silent, still and deep.

Springtime broke from the morning sky's purple glow and there you were, a new radiance shining in your eyes like day's light at dawn's creation.

I saw all, and all was one. The precious image of my eternal Friend, a reflection of heaven's radiance was all around. My heart was full. Radiant light, your words do not deceive. In the desert I saw all of you. Wherever fate may lead me, this happiness will not fade away.

And yet in an instant, all was gone. On the horizon was rising the sun. Stillness was in the desert, but in the morning light I heard within the echo of distant bells.

Solovyev's great vision of Divine Sophia in the Egyptian desert became the central motivation and impulse for his whole life's work as a philosopher, as a true friend of Sophia. He was dedicated to teaching philosophy to the Russian people, and to working for the reunification of the Eastern and Western Churches. Solovyev believed it was a scandal for Christianity that the Church was divided, and he felt that through Sophia there could be a reunification between East and West. Sadly, during his lifetime, Solovyev's dreams did not materialize, and he was disappointed in his labors. However, his great impulse to work for peace and unity among all Christians lives on, and in the twentieth century there finally emerged an ecumenical movement toward unity. So his work was not in vain.

Solovyev was a great prophet of the New Age, of the age that is beginning in the twenty-first century, the age of the inflowing of the Divine Feminine. Solovyev inspired many in Russia, among them poets and theologians. Through him the tradition now known as Sophiology, the science or the theology of Sophia, came to birth in Russia through Russian Orthodox priests who took up Solovyev's work and carried it further. Solovyev was not only a great philosopher. He was also a great poet, who described Sophia in the following way:

As the living center or soul of all creatures,
She includes the manifoldness of living souls.

She is all of humanity together in one, or the soul of the world.
She is ideal humanity, containing all individual living creatures
or souls and uniting them through herself.
Her task is to mediate and unify the manifoldness of living
creatures, who constitute the actual content of her life and the
absolute unity of God.

Solovyev saw Sophia as the soul of the world, having three aspects, which allow her to unify, connect, and direct everything. She possesses a higher divine part, a lower earthly part, and a middle part, which creates and directs space, time, and causality. In his description of Sophia as the soul of the world, Solovyev writes:

If the soul of the world were to stop unifying everything through
herself, all created beings would lose their common relationship.
The union of the cosmos would fall apart into a multiplicity of
individual elements, and the organism of the world would
transform itself into a mechanical mass of atoms.

Lastly, here is a short poem about Sophia entitled "Today I Saw Her":

Today I saw her with my eyes.
My queen all bathed in radiance.
Rejoicing, my heart stopped beating.
This happened at the golden light of dawn,
A miracle divine.
All earthly desire vanished,
Seeing her alone, her alone, only her.

Vladimir Solovyev is the last great nineteenth-century herald in the Sophia tradition extending from St. Hildegard of Bingen through Jakob Boehme and down to the modern age. In Solovyev we find an illumined mind, a great philosopher and poet, and one whose will was inspired to bring about peace between all Christians. Vladimir Solovyev's life and work stands as an inspiring example to us all.

We have followed the Sophia tradition in the West from the time of the incarnation of Christ. And we have seen that, despite holding back from mainstream Christian development over the past two thousand years, Divine Sophia continued to reveal herself to certain chosen individuals culminating with Vladimir Solovyev in the nineteenth century. Now, in the twenty-first century, the first century of a new millennium, we can see a turning point, a beginning of a New Age in which Sophia is beginning to reveal herself to more and more human beings. In the next section of the book, I would like to begin to look in closer detail at this New Age. It is relevant to every human being on this planet, because Divine Sophia is now able to form a personal relationship with each and every human being in the unfolding of her revelation of the New Age.

A Spiritual Practice to Invoke Divine Sophia

In the twenty-first century we need to find a different kind of relationship to the wisdom of Divine Sophia. A spiritual practice that I have found immensely helpful in this regard was taught by the spiritual teacher I mentioned in the Introduction—Valentin Tomberg, the Russian author of the manuscript I translated. Valentin Tomberg was born in St. Petersburg in 1900 and died on the island of Majorca in 1973, having emigrated to the West after the Bolshevik Revolution. He was a teacher of the Sophia mysteries and of esoteric

Christianity, and taught a prayer which helps to bring to realization within oneself the birth of the divine I AM. Actually, it is the traditional prayer directed to the Virgin Mary but now understood in the sense of Sophia as the higher wisdom that manifested through Mary two thousand years ago.

This prayer, the *Hail Mary,* in Latin the *Ave Maria,* was given to humanity through the Virgin Mary, and next to the *Lord's Prayer* is one of the most popular prayers in Christianity. The words of the *Hail Mary* actually derive from the Gospel of St. Luke, which notes that at the time of the Annunciation the Archangel Gabriel appeared to Mary and spoke the following words:

Hail Mary, full of grace, the Lord is with thee.
Blessed art thou among women, and blessed is the fruit of thy
womb.

The divine revelation communicated to Mary by the Archangel Gabriel was the good news, awaited for centuries by the Jewish people, of the conception of Jesus as the Christ or Logos. The prayer continues with our response, as human beings, to this great event: *Holy Mary, Mother of God, pray for us now and in the hour of our death.*

Valentin Tomberg took the basic structure of this prayer, which has a mantric quality, and brought into its context not only the birth of Jesus the man, but of Christ as the divine I AM. In the Gospel of St. John can be found seven I AM affirmations related to Jesus Christ. Tomberg describes these seven I AM affirmations as seven Christian mantras relating to the seven lotus flowers or the seven chakra centers in each human being. These chakras are known and described in different spiritual and esoteric traditions as the centers of higher organs of knowledge and perception. These seven centers relate to the soul-astral body of the human being. They are subtle centers, located respectively in the vicinity of the crown of the head, the center of the forehead, the larynx, the region of the heart, the solar plexus, the abdomen, and the base of the spine. These seven chakras are centers that are to be awakened on the path of spiritual development, and this awakening brings with it new spiritual faculties and perceptions.

Valentin Tomberg describes these centers and their different functions, and he provides a way of incorporating the I AM affirmations as Christian mantras into the form of the *Hail Mary* prayer. For example, *I AM the resurrection and the life* is the I AM affirmation or Christian mantra to awaken the crown chakra. When we meditate on the words *I AM the resurrection and the life* in connection with the crown chakra we activate an actual ray or vibration that can help to awaken the spiritual faculties connected with it. The words *I AM the light of the world* are the Christian mantra to awaken the spiritual potential in the chakra at the center of the forehead. When we meditate on the words *I AM the light of the world* the chakra in the center of the forehead, which is conceived as having two petals, can become awakened, and the two petals can be opened up to become organs of communication with higher spiritual beings. Each of the seven chakras has its own spiritual potential that can be awakened when we use the correct mantra.

Briefly, each I AM affirmation is conceived as a ray from the divine I AM, Jesus Christ. If we hold up a prism before a light source, we see the light become fragmented into seven rays corresponding to the seven colors of the rainbow. In the same way we can conceive of the seven I AM affirmations as seven revelations of Christ, the divine I AM. We might also visualize these seven rays proceeding from

Christ as the divine I AM, each ray then becoming active in a different center in the human being. In this spiritual practice we contemplate the seven I AM affirmations in turn and in relation to their corresponding chakras.

Clairvoyants who behold the chakras describe them as having the form of lotus flowers, the lotus being one of the most beautiful flowers. The chakras as lotus flowers are structured such that each has a different number of petals. For example, as we have seen, the center in the forehead is described as the two-petaled lotus flower, whose petals can become organs of reception of spiritual impulses from higher realms. The center at the crown of the head is referred to in the Oriental tradition as the thousand-petaled lotus. Tomberg describes this center as having eight petals that are in such rapid and scintillating movement that there actually appear to be a thousand petals.

Further, he describes the chakra center in the region of the larynx as a lotus flower with sixteen petals, four petals extending upwards for the inflowing revelation from above, four petals extending to the right, four to the left, and four extending down toward the heart chakra. When this lotus flower is brought into movement the petals begin to rotate. Tomberg states that there is one complete rotation of the sixteen-petaled lotus flower in the period of one hour, and that it is activated through meditating upon the words *I AM the good shepherd.*

The heart center is described as having twelve petals, and the corresponding I AM affirmation for this center is *I AM the bread of life.* Meditating upon these words helps to activate the heart center to open to its true spiritual potential. Moving down lower to the solar plexus we find the ten-petaled lotus flower that is awakened through the Christian mantra *I AM the door.* At the level of the abdomen is found the six-petaled lotus flower, and its relevant I AM statement is *I AM the way, the truth, and the life.* Lastly, we come to the chakra at the base of the spine, often referred to as the root chakra, which has four petals. The I AM statement for this center is *I AM the true vine.* These are the seven I AM statements which represent seven revelations of different aspects of the divine I AM. As we have seen, each I AM affirmation relates to one of the seven chakras.

In the *Hail Mary*, each I AM affirmation is brought into the prayer, which is repeated seven times, each time with a different I AM focus. In Tomberg's description of this practice we begin at the top with the crown chakra and the words *I AM the resurrection and the life.* We proceed down then to the forehead chakra with the words *I AM the light of the world* and so on. In this spiritual practice, which is a powerful meditation and prayer, we proceed through the seven chakras in descending order from the crown to the root chakra. This sets a spiritual current in motion corresponding to the stream of the washing of the feet. It represents the bringing down of pure spiritual light and warmth from the crown chakra down to the root chakra and then sending it on down through the feet and into Earth. This is a very powerful practice of spiritual purification.

Before going through this prayer of the Hail Mary with its seven I AM affirmations, let us place it in context. Let us imagine this great event of the Annunciation two thousand years ago. The Virgin Mary, who was very young at the time—about fourteen and a half years old—was at home in Nazareth. One night the mighty archangel Gabriel appears to her. This scene has been portrayed in numerous paintings of the Annunciation, especially by Fra Angelico, who depicted it many times. What actually took place? That night is honored as holy

74

for it saw the conception of the child Jesus as a spiritual event, where the Virgin Mary opened to receive the incoming, incarnating soul of Jesus. This is the significance of the Annunciation. And now, if we take the *Hail Mary* prayer as a new spiritual practice in our own time, each human being who offers this prayer to Divine Sophia as the mother of humanity and the regent of his or her own soul asks Sophia to bring to birth within them the divine I AM presence of the Christ. Through this prayer, the I AM presence can incarnate into us so that our soul is permeated through and through by Christ. In this way, the I AM presence descends through the seven chakras—the organs of our soul—bringing them alive through each I AM affirmation.

Some people call this Sophianic spiritual practice the *Little Rosary*. The word rosary means garland of roses. In the East, each chakra is described as a lotus flower, this being the most beautiful expression of the flower kingdom. In the West, we tend to give this high place to the rose, and we might think of the chakras as a garland of seven roses. The term *Little Rosary* describes our new spiritual practice, in contrast to the *Great Rosary* of the Catholic tradition, which consists of fifty *Hail Marys*.

This prayer, the *Little Rosary*, is not exactly in the form that Valentin Tomberg originally gave it, but is the form that emerged for me working with it over many years in connection with eurythmy as an art of spiritual movement. However, it can be offered without combining it with eurythmy. It can be prayed at any time of day, although a particularly wonderful time is late evening when the Annunciation to Mary actually took place. The significance of the relationship between the I AM affirmations and the corresponding chakras is something upon which we can meditate and reflect.

For example, the words *I AM the light of the world*, which corre-
spond to the two-petaled chakra at the center of the forehead,
obviously have to do with our ability to see with this organ that is
called the third eye. And so the words *I AM the light of the world* shine
into the third eye to bring about the power of spiritual seeing. It
bestows a seeing that goes beyond what we can see with our two eyes
in the natural world, and enables us to begin to see by means of the
Spirit-Sun of existence, the divine I AM. This is one example, but one
can ponder the deeper significance of the correspondence between the
I AM affirmations and every one of the seven chakras

You might now wish to pray the *Little Rosary*, calling upon Divine
Sophia as the mother of humanity, to bring the Divine Logos, the I
AM, the power of divine love and divine light to illuminate and warm
your soul.

Hail Mary, full of grace, the Lord is with thee.
Blessed art thou among women, and blessed is the fruit of thy
womb, Jesus Christ, who speaks:
Crown *I AM the resurrection and the life.*
Holy Mary, mother of God,
Pray for us now, and in the hour of our death.

Hail Mary, full of grace, the Lord is with thee.
Blessed art thou among women, and blessed is the fruit of thy
womb, Jesus Christ, who speaks:
3rd Eye *I AM the light of the world.*
Holy Mary, mother of God,
Pray for us now, and in the hour of our death.

Hail Mary, full of grace, the Lord is with thee.
Blessed art thou among women, and blessed is the fruit of thy
womb, Jesus Christ, who speaks:
throat *I AM the good shepherd.*
Holy Mary, mother of God,
Pray for us now, and in the hour of our death.

Hail Mary, full of grace, the Lord is with thee.
Blessed art thou among women, and blessed is the fruit of thy
womb, Jesus Christ, who speaks:
Heart *I AM the bread of life.*
Holy Mary, mother of God,
Pray for us now, and in the hour of our death.

Hail Mary, full of grace, the Lord is with thee.
Blessed art thou among women, and blessed is the fruit of thy
womb, Jesus Christ, who speaks:
Solar
Plexus *I AM the door, the entrance and the exit.*
Holy Mary, mother of God,
Pray for us now, and in the hour of our death.

Hail Mary, full of grace, the Lord is with thee.
Blessed art thou among women, and blessed is the fruit of thy
womb, Jesus Christ, who speaks:
Lower
abdo *I AM the way, the truth, and the life.*
Holy Mary, mother of God,
Pray for us now, and in the hour of our death.

Hail Mary, full of grace, the Lord is with thee.
Blessed art thou among women, and blessed is the fruit of thy
womb, Jesus Christ, who speaks:
Root *I AM the true vine.*
Holy Mary, mother of God,
Pray for us now, and in the hour of our death.

Amen.

Chapter Five
The Influence of Divine
Sophia in the East

W E HAVE SEEN HOW DIVINE SOPHIA HAS revealed herself to certain European mystics during the past thousand years. Interestingly, the Sophia teachings had a profound influence in the East. And the mystery of the Palladium leads us back to the East. What happened to the Palladium after its recapture from Troy?

The Palladium was a wooden statue of Pallas Athena, three cubits high, which, like the Kaaba in Mecca, had at its center a meteor that was believed to have fallen from heaven. This meteoric component is said to have conferred invulnerability upon the possessor of the Palladium. Buried in the depths below the city, guarded by vestal virgins, the Palladium was the source of the power of the city of Troy. But Troy lost its invulnerability when Odysseus, disguised as a beggar, secretly entered the city and recaptured the meteoric component of the Palladium. By this act, Odysseus literally opened the door to the destruction of the city of Troy, because, due to the skillful maneuvering of Odysseus, the Greeks were able to enter the city and set fire to it.

In the light of this Greek victory, it is somewhat of a surprise to learn that the Trojan priest Aeneas rescued the wooden statue of the Palladium from the flames and thus prevented it from falling into Greek hands. The travels of Aeneas, recorded in the *Aeneid*, tell us of the further destiny of the Palladium. After leaving Troy, Aeneas traveled around the Mediterranean and eventually came to the region of present-day Rome, where he married the daughter of the Roman king, Latinus. And so the Palladium came to rest in Rome, where, as in Troy, a special temple was built for it beneath the city, guarded by vestal virgins. In this underground temple an eternally burning flame gave the city of Rome its power over the whole of the ancient world. In the second century CE the emperor Trajan brought from Egypt a colossal porphyry pillar from the temple of Isis and had it placed above the underground temple of the Palladium.

In the fourth century CE, the emperor Constantine the Great heard the prophecy of the sibyls that the city of Rome would collapse and its power would be lost. In an attempt to secure the future of the Empire, he decided to transfer the capital from Rome to Constantinople, the city named after him, with the idea of creating an even greater empire embracing the East and the West. Constantine the Great carried out his bold plan and transferred the Palladium to Constantinople, where it was placed once again in an underground temple guarded by vestal virgins. The colossal porphyry pillar from the temple of Isis was also transported to Constantinople and placed above the Palladium.

The Palladium is a Sophianic symbol. Let us recall that the Palladium was given to Ilias, the founder of Troy, by Athena, Greek goddess of wisdom. Through the power of the Palladium we have a Sun symbol, a burning light of wisdom beneath the earth that confers power upon its possessor. The light of that wisdom now radiated forth from Constantinople. On top of the porphyry pillar from the temple of Isis the emperor Constantine had placed a golden statue of Apollo, but he had the face of Apollo made in his own likeness. Thus we can see that Constantine suffered from megalomania. He then created a halo around this golden statue of Apollo, a halo made from some nails and wood from the cross upon which Christ had been crucified in Jerusalem. These precious relics had been brought back from Jerusalem to Constantinople by Constantine's mother Helen. Constantine adorned his statue with this inscription: *That which sheds its beneficial influence here shall, like the Sun, endure for all time, and proclaim the fame of its founder, Constantine, for all eternity.*

Constantine's inscription did not live up to its promise. A few centuries later, the statue was struck by lightning and half the pillar was destroyed. The rest of it still stands to the present day in the city of Istanbul, the current name for Constantinople. And, it is said, the Palladium is still buried beneath this pillar. We await, therefore, with great interest any clues to the future destiny of the Palladium. The meteor from the Palladium was taken by Odysseus to Greece. But that's a whole other story.

Early in the twentieth century some followers of Rudolf Steiner went to Istanbul and began excavations there to locate the Palladium, but without success. According to legend, the Palladium will one day be recovered and transferred to a Slavic kingdom in the north, to Russia. This points to the coming Aquarian Age in which, it is said, there will be a new culture, of which present-day Russia is the first sign—a culture that will blossom and flourish under the inspiration of Divine Sophia. This points to a Christianity of the New Age, what we might call a Sophianic Christianity, that will arise and flourish in Russia and the other Slavic countries. This is the great promise for the future.

We might ask: What signs are there of a Sophianic Christianity in Russia? One of the greatest monuments to Christianity is the great basilica of Hagia Sophia, constructed by Emperor Justinian in Constantinople. For a long time Hagia Sophia possessed the largest dome in the world, and its very name means Holy Sophia. Justinian was of the school that viewed Sophia as identical with the Logos, the Christ. So the Hagia Sophia in Constantinople, built not far from the site of the Palladium, is really a basilica dedicated to Christ as the wisdom of the world.

When Christianity spread to Russia in the year 988 CE its orientation was not to the Roman Catholic world but to the Greek Orthodox tradition centered at Constantinople. The great temple of Holy Sophia in Constantinople also provided inspiration for the Russians, but they interpreted Sophia not as the Logos or Christ but as Divine Sophia the feminine side of God, the feminine messenger of the Divine. Hagia Sophia was the archetype for Russian cathedrals such as the Holy Sophia cathedrals in Kiev and in Novgorod, built in the middle of the eleventh century. The very fact that the festival days of these two cathedrals are identical with the celebration of the birth of the Virgin Mary (Kiev) and of the Ascension of the Virgin Mary (Novgorod) points to this relationship with the Divine Feminine. So from the very beginning of Christianity in Russia and Ukraine, we find a true Sophianic quality entering in with the construction of these cathedrals dedicated to Holy Sophia.

Another testimony to the nature of worship and devotion to Sophia in Russia is to be found in the Russian icon tradition. In Novgorod we find the great icon of Divine Sophia, a majestic representation of Sophia as an angelic being seated upon a throne, radiating her rays of wisdom to all humanity. To her right is the Virgin Mary, to her left is John the Baptist, as the two human beings closest to Divine Sophia. Above her is the risen Christ, and above him the open book of the sacred word representing the Word of God. This inspiring icon of Sophia is found in different parts of Russia and is further testimony of the Russian people's dedication to Divine Sophia.

Sophia has been at the root of Russian Orthodox Christianity, even though within the Russian Church itself there was little understanding on a conscious level of the nature of Divine Sophia, until the time of the philosopher and mystic Solovyev in the nineteenth century. Before that time, what we find is an instinctive worship of Divine Sophia in the Russian Orthodox Church. However, we can be grateful to the Russian Orthodox Church for having preserved this Sophianic influence that disappeared by and large from the Western Church. The presence of the Divine Sophia in the Russian Orthodox tradition itself points to the future Sophianic culture that will emerge in Russia.

Vladimir Solovyev was the first within the Russian Orthodox tradition to reveal, on a conscious level, the mystery of Divine Sophia as the world soul, the mother, guide, and inspiration of future humanity. Following Solovyev, we find two key figures in the development of Russian Sophiology. These two are the Russian Orthodox priests, Pavel Florensky and Sergei Bulgakov.

Florensky was born in 1882 in Tiflis in Georgia and was from youth an extraordinarily gifted child. He was a brilliant mathematician, yet he became a priest. When the Bolsheviks came to power in the Soviet Union they planned to bring electricity to those vast lands, and, although he was a priest, Florensky was enlisted to help with this great project due to his mathematical abilities. Florensky continued to wear his priestly robes and his great cross, and this, of course, was an unusual sight in the Soviet Union. He wore his priestly garb when he spoke at the Soviet Academy of Sciences in the year 1926. It was tolerated at the time but, later, Florensky was viciously attacked by Stalin. In the 1930s, he was sent to a concentration camp on the White Islands in the far north of Russia where he was executed in 1937.

Florensky suffered an ignominious end, but now in contemporary Russia he is regarded as a hero and has even been called the "Leonardo" of Russian culture. He was a truly spiritual individual, with a brilliant mind and a heart devoted to the divine. His major work on Sophia is called *The Pillar and Foundation of Truth*. In this work he describes Sophia as the soul of the world:

This sublime, royal and feminine nature who is not God or the eternal Son, nor an angel or one of the saints: Is she not the true synthesis of all humanity, the higher and more complete form of the world, the living soul of nature and the universe?

He continues:

Sophia is the grand root of the synthesis of everything that is created, that is, the entire creation and not just all creatures.

Sophia is the guardian angel, the ideal person of the world, its formational foundation.

Florensky's Sophia teachings are drawn from the Russian Orthodox tradition, from the tradition of the whole Church back to its foundation, and from the Books of Wisdom from the Old Testament. Florensky tried to find a pure teaching of Sophia that would be acceptable within the Russian Orthodox Church. In this respect Florensky differs from Solovyev, who incorporated teachings of the mystics such as Jakob Boehme. Florensky focussed upon a purely Christian interpretation of Sophia from the Christian tradition without including any gnostic elements such as we find in Jakob Boehme's work. Florensky also pointed to the central significance of the Virgin Mary as a manifestation and incarnation of the Divine Sophia. Concerning the relationship between Mary and Sophia, Florensky writes:

Sophia is the first created and the first redeemed, the heart of redeemed creation. She is the Church, that is, the whole of everyone who comes to enjoy redemption and makes up the body of Christ. Sophia is personal virginity, that is, the power which makes a human being entirely whole. Mary carries this virginal power in her par excellence. She is, therefore, the manifestation of Sophia, that is, Sophia incarnated.

Thus, although Florensky came to this perspective independently, his views concerning Mary as the incarnated Sophia are identical with the teaching of Jakob Boehme.

Florensky was a personal friend of the Russian priest Sergei Bulgakov (1871–1944), perhaps the most prodigious of the Sophianic theologians. At the time of the Bolshevik Revolution, Bulgakov was exiled from Russia and went to live in France, where he later became head of the Russian Orthodox Seminary in Paris. Bulgakov dedicated his life to expounding his teachings concerning Sophia, and his works comprise the most comprehensive body of knowledge on Sophiology. Bulgakov's purpose was, like Florensky, to present Sophia in a way that would be acceptable to his fellow priests and theologians of the Russian Orthodox Church. In this, as with Florensky, Bulgakov did not derive anything of his teaching from Gnostic sources outside of the Church, but concentrated solely upon the Church tradition. Nevertheless, in his exposition of the nature of Divine Sophia, Bulgakov later ran into conflict with the Moscow authorities and he was condemned on account of his Sophia teachings.

What was it about Bulgakov's views of Sophia that caused him to become viewed as a heretic? It was his idea that Sophia is the *ousia* (to use the Greek word), the substance that is common to the three persons of the Holy Trinity—the Father, the Son, and the Holy Spirit. This idea aroused the suspicion within Bulgakov's fellow theologians that Sophia could be put forward as a fourth hypostasis alongside the Father, the Son, and the Holy Spirit. However, let us hear what Bulgakov himself says concerning this idea of Sophia as the *ousia* or substance common to the Holy Trinity. Bulgakov wrote:

> *The three divine persons of the Holy Trinity have a life in common, that is, an* ousia, *Sophia. However, this does not mean transforming the Trinity into a Quaternity.*

Here Bulgakov denies that the idea of Sophia being the common life of the Holy Trinity would transform it into a Quaternity. Nevertheless, it was for this that he was condemned. This did not affect Bulgakov's position as the head of the Russian Orthodox Seminary in Paris. He continued to write and carry out his functions as a priest, but from this time onward his writings bore the stigma of heresy.

I was present in 1996 at a Sophia conference in Rome, to which Russian theologians as well as Roman Catholic priests and theologians had been invited. The theme of this conference was "Sophia as the Bridge between East and West." I learned that up to the present time within the Russian Orthodox Church the teachings of Bulgakov were still regarded as heretical. I also learned there is hope within the Russian Orthodox Church that there will one day be a great council dedicated to Sophia. First held by Solovyev, the dream to unite East and West still persists.

Russian Sophiology, a rich theological and philosophical tradition founded by Solovyev, and continued by Florensky and Bulgakov, suffered great setbacks under the communist regime of Stalin and awaits a full re-emergence in the future.

Valentin Tomberg
Valentin Tomberg was of central significance for the Russian Sophia tradition, and he carried it a stage further. It is my conviction that he represents the pinnacle of the Sophianic tradition in Russia up until the present time. I believe his teachings will occupy humanity for millennia, just as the teaching of the Holy Trinity within the Christian tradition occupied theologians from the fourth century down to the present time.

What are his teachings concerning the Divine Sophia? We can enter into them if we first review Florensky's views and see how Valentin Tomberg's teachings go a stage further and completely transform them. According to Florensky, based on the Wisdom Books of the Old Testament, Sophia is a created being, the first created being. And as the first created being she is the highest created being of all existence. Being the very first created being, she came forth from the womb of the Holy Trinity, and therefore has a relationship to each member of the Holy Trinity. In the eyes of Florensky, Divine Sophia as the first created being has a relationship to the Father, the Son, and the Holy Spirit. Florensky states:

Sophia participates in the life of the Trihypostatic Godhead. She enters into the bosom of the Trinity and she partakes of Divine Love. But, being a fourth *created person she does not "constitute" Divine Unity, nor is "Love," but only enters into the communion Love and is allowed to enter into this communion by the ineffable, unfathomable, unthinkable humility of God. From the point of view of the* Father, *Sophia is the ideal* substance, *the foundation of creation, the power or force of its being. If we turn to the Son, the Word, then Sophia is the* reason *of creation, its meaning, truth or justice. And lastly, from the point of view of the Holy Spirit, we find in Sophia the* spirituality *of creation, its holiness, purity and immaculateness, that is, its beauty.*

Florensky here elaborates three aspects of Sophia as the first created being. The first aspect is that of Sophia as the original substance of the creation in her relationship to the Father. Secondly,

Matrix

88

that Sophia is the wisdom of creation in relationship to the Son, to the Word. Thirdly, that Sophia is the beauty and spirituality of creation in relation to the Holy Spirit. Tomberg goes a stage further, in that he speaks of Sophia not simply as having three aspects but of Sophia as being three *persons*. He speaks of a Sophianic Trinity parallel or complementary to the Holy Trinity. In this profound teaching, the Divine Feminine is a Trinity comprising the Mother, who complements the Father, the Daughter who complements the Son, and the Holy Soul who is the counterpart of the Holy Spirit. This Divine Feminine Trinity is thus another side of the Godhead, complementary to the masculine Trinity of the Godhead of Father, Son, and Holy Spirit.

In order to contemplate some of the far-reaching implications of Valentin Tomberg's Sophia teachings, let us dwell for a moment on this Sophianic Trinity of Mother, Daughter, and Holy Soul. How can we conceive of this Trinity? Astronomers nowadays consider the act of creation as occurring at a definite moment in time and speak of it as the Big Bang. I do not subscribe to the Big Bang theory, but I would say that if we go back far enough there is indeed a definite beginning to the coming into existence of creation. However, if we go back prior to this time, what would we find? There would be the Godhead, the original Primordial Being, who is neither masculine nor feminine, the Creator, who is the Primordial Being of all existence. At the moment when the creation begins, however, we find a polarization taking place within this Primordial Being of the Godhead, a polarization into that part of the Godhead that goes into the Creation and that part of the Godhead that remains transcendental to the Creation.

In philosophical terms, we have, therefore, a transcendental aspect and an immanent aspect of the Godhead. In the light of the Sophia teachings, the transcendental aspect would be called the Father. The immanent aspect of the Godhead would be called the Mother. The word Mother itself conveys something of this. The Latin for mother is *mater* and the Latin word for matter is *materia*. We find, therefore, that the Mother can be conceived as the primordial substance of all creation. In the polarization within the Godhead at the beginning of creation, we find we can differentiate between the Creation, that is the Divine Mother, and that which is transcendental to the Creation, that is, the Divine Father.

Valentin Tomberg teaches that arising out of the primordial Godhead begotten from the Divine Father and the Divine Mother are the Divine Son and the Divine Daughter, Christ and Sophia, the Logos and Sophia. As the Word and the Wisdom of creation, the Divine Son and the Divine Daughter worked for eons of time in shaping the primordial matter of existence in order to bring forth the world as we know it, the world created through the wisdom of Sophia and the fire of the Divine Logos. In this Sophianic teaching, therefore, we find the Son and the Daughter of the Divine who work together in the formation of the world and humanity.

And, just as we may understand that the incarnation of the Logos, Christ, took place in Jesus, so, according to Jakob Boehme and the Russian Sophiologists, there also took place an incarnation of Divine Sophia into Mary. And just as the incarnation of the Logos, the Christ, into Jesus took place at the baptism in the Jordan, so, according to Valentin Tomberg, the incarnation of Sophia into Mary took place at the event of Pentecost. Having prayed throughout the night together, the disciples gathered around Mary on Pentecost

Sunday morning. On that holy day there took place the incarnation of Sophia into Mary, making possible the descent of the Holy Spirit, depicted as tongues of fire, above the heads of the disciples.

Having followed the unfolding of the Divine Feminine in relation to the Divine Masculine, let us consider the next stage, namely the relationship of the Holy Spirit on the one hand to the Father and to the Son, and on the other hand of the Holy Soul in relation to the Divine Mother and the Divine Daughter. In Christian theology, the Holy Spirit is conceived as weaving between the Father and the Son. The Divine Father is conceived as being at rest outside of the Creation, while the Divine Son, having incarnated into a human body upon Earth, is seen as having entered into the center, into the heart of creation. Between the Cross of Golgotha and the Father, transcendent to all creation, weaves the Holy Spirit as the one who renews and revitalizes all that is living. The Holy Spirit is conceived of as one who enlightens, leading humanity onward to ever-higher levels of spiritual consciousness.

Let us now consider the Divine Feminine Trinity of the Mother, the Daughter and the Holy Soul. The Divine Mother is essentially the whole of creation, embracing all the stars, planets, Sun, Moon, the Earth, and all living creatures. Valentin Tomberg teaches that the heart of the Divine Mother is to be found in the center of the Earth and that the plant kingdom resonates with the very heartbeat of the Mother. The Divine Daughter is the wisdom of the cosmos, pictured as the soul of the world embracing the entire cosmos extending from the realm of the fixed stars down to the planets and the Moon. This awe-inspiring image of Sophia as the world soul can be found in the Book of Revelation, where, as I mentioned earlier in the book, she is depicted as a woman clothed with the Sun, with the Moon under her feet, and upon her head a crown of twelve stars.

Between the Divine Mother in the center of the Earth and the Divine Daughter Sophia as the world soul, weaves the Holy Soul, the third aspect of the Divine Feminine Trinity. The Holy Soul is the creator of community, who ensouls and elevates groups of human beings in the progress of unfolding evolution. We find an example of this in the spiritual tradition of Israel that conceives of the Shekinah as the soul of the community of Israel. Here Shekinah corresponds to the Holy Soul weaving between the Divine Daughter and the Divine Mother. In this Sophia teaching of the Divine Feminine Trinity— Mother, Daughter, and Holy Soul—we reach the pinnacle of the Sophia tradition of Russia. This central teaching of the Divine Feminine Trinity will be a source of inspiration for seekers of divine wisdom in the coming ages, just as the teaching of the Holy Trinity— Father, Son, and Holy Spirit—has been a source of inspiration for Christians in ages past. Valentin Tomberg arrived at an extraordinary understanding of the Divine Feminine synthesized in these three persons—Mother, Daughter, and Holy Soul.

Spiritual Practices to Invoke Divine Sophia

How can we understand the Trinity of the Divine Feminine more profoundly? I suggest beginning with a wonderful prayer directed to the Divine Mother, the *Our Mother* prayer. Valentin Tomberg introduced this prayer to a small circle of his pupils during the Second World War.

> *Our Mother, thou who art in the darkness of the underworld,*
> *May the holiness of thy name shine anew in our remembering.*

May the breath of thy awakening kingdom warm the hearts of all who wander homeless.

May the resurrection of thy will renew eternal faith even unto the depths of physical substance.

Receive this day the living memory of thee from human hearts,

Who implore thee to forgive the sin of forgetting thee,

And who are ready to fight against temptation which has led thee to existence in darkness,

That through the deed of the Son the immeasurable pain of the Father be stilled,

By the liberation of all beings from the tragedy of thy withdrawal.

For thine is the homeland and the boundless wisdom, and the all-merciful grace,

For all and everything in the circle of all.

Amen.

This prayer, the *Our Mother*, corresponds to the *Our Father*, the *Lord's Prayer*, in that it has seven petitions. The *Our Father* starts off with the words: *Our Father, who art in Heaven.* The *Our Mother* begins with the words: *Our Mother, thou who art in the darkness of the underworld.* Here immediately our attention is drawn to the polarity of the Divine Father who is the transcendental being of all creation and the Divine Mother who is the immanent being of all creation.

The *Our Father* continues with the first petition: *Hallowed be thy name.* The first petition of the *Our Mother* prayer begins: *May the holiness of thy name shine anew in our remembering.* Here is reference to the name of the Divine Mother. To the Greeks she was Demeter, in the Orient she was called the Great Mother, Magna Mater, to the

Egyptians she was Isis. The name of the Divine Mother should begin to shine anew in our remembering, for we have forgotten her during the course of the last two thousand years.

With the *Our Father* the second petition is: *Thy kingdom come.* The second petition of the *Our Mother* prayer refers to the divine kingdom of the Mother: *May the breath of thy awakening kingdom warm the hearts of all who wander homeless.* This refers to the kingdom of the Divine Mother, the realm that is referred to as Shambhala in the East, this lost kingdom of paradise, this golden realm that has sunk down to the center of the Earth. We find references in different mythologies and spiritual traditions that at one time humanity dwelt in paradise together with the whole being of nature, and with the four streams of life forces flowing through the being of the Divine Mother. Since the Fall, the paradise of Shambhala has been lost and has sunk down into the depths of the Earth. But now in our time it is possible to find a new access to this kingdom of the Divine Mother.

The third petition of the *Our Father, Thy will be done on earth as it is in heaven,* is mirrored in the *Our Mother* with the words: *May the resurrection of thy will renew eternal faith even unto the depths of physical substance.* Here is a reference to the divine will of the Mother, which is eternally faithful to the Father in the heights. The divine will of the Mother is one day to become reunited with the Father, and this event will signify the complete transubstantiation and spiritualizing of the Earth, which will, in the future, create a new paradise or kingdom of heaven.

In the fourth petition of the *Our Father* are the words: *Give us this day our daily bread.* The fourth petition of the *Our Mother* prayer is: *Receive this day the living memory of thee from human hearts.* In this fourth petition our attention is drawn to the fact that we are alive and sustained through the grace of the Divine Mother. With every breath we take, the food we eat, the water we drink, we are continually supported by Mother Earth, the Divine Mother. Now is the time to acknowledge our debt of gratitude to the Divine Mother for her ever-present support and unconditional love.

In the fifth petition of the *Lord's Prayer* the words are: *Forgive us our trespasses as we forgive those who trespass against us.* The fifth petition of the *Our Mother* is: *Who implore thee to forgive the sin of forgetting thee.* Here we are reminded that in forgetting the Divine Mother during the last two thousand years we have committed a sin of omission and we implore her to forgive us. Now is the time when the Divine Mother needs to return into our consciousness, and needs to be acknowledged.

In the sixth petition of the *Lord's Prayer* are the words: *Lead us not into temptation.* In the *Our Mother* prayer the corresponding petition is: *And are ready to fight against temptation which has led thee to existence in darkness.* Here is a reference to the original temptation that took place in paradise, in the Garden of Eden. Through succumbing to that temptation, humanity experienced the Fall, and out of love for humanity the whole of nature also experienced the Fall. Our task now is to resist temptation. The primary temptation of our time is that of humanity, through technology, dominating Mother Earth, and compelling her to give more than she is able to freely bestow on us. We have to resist this temptation to dominate and to plunder, for this holds the Divine Mother in darkness and obscurity. We have to learn to begin to live again in harmony with Mother Earth, to include her in our thoughts, our feelings, and our deeds.

In the seventh petition of the *Lord's Prayer* are the words: *But deliver us from evil.* The corresponding seventh petition to the *Our Mother* is: *That through the deed of the Son the immeasurable pain of the Father be stilled by the liberation of all beings from the tragedy of thy withdrawal.* Here the focus is not upon our deliverance from evil, but on the liberation of all the beings of nature who have suffered through the Fall and through the consequent withdrawal of the heart of the Divine Mother into the depths. This event, the Fall, has given rise to pain and suffering on the part of the Father, and it is the deed of the Son, Christ, to work in overcoming this Fall of humanity. The mystery that is conveyed after Christ's death on the Cross is his descent into the underworld to the Mother, where he implants in the womb of the Earth the seeds for the Earth's redemption. This deed of Christ can be an inspiration for all human beings to participate in the raising up and redemption of the entire Earth.

What I am speaking of here is hardly known in the Christian tradition, where the focus is upon the death on the Cross and then the resurrection. The death on the Cross took place on Good Friday. The descent into the underworld took place on Easter Saturday, the resurrection on Easter Sunday. It has been a mystery up until the twentieth century as to what really took place on Easter Saturday with the descent of Christ into the underworld. By and large, this mystery could not have been understood by humanity in earlier times. The unveiling of this mystery signifies an opening to the mysteries of the Divine Feminine that have become accessible in the twentieth century through the teachings of individuals such as Valentin Tomberg. The descent into the underworld to the Divine Mother is the counterpart to the Ascension forty days after the Resurrection, the Ascension of Christ to the realm of the Father. This is the polarity. We can see that through the descent to the Mother, and the subsequent ascent to the Father, Christ worked to reunite the Father and the Mother. This is a profound mystery—the work of the Son is to overcome the chasm that occurred at the time of the Fall with the descent of the heart of the Mother into the underworld.

Chapter Six
Modern Teachings of Sophia

O THER TEACHERS IN THE NINETEENTH AND twentieth centuries have referred to the mystery of the Divine Mother. One of the most significant was Madame Helena Blavatsky, who was born in Russia in 1831 and died in 1891. Madame Blavatsky is remembered as the founder of the Theosophical Society in New York in 1875. The word *Theosophy* itself points to the Divine Sophia, *Theo-Sophia*, the wisdom of God. Blavatsky had a special task to open up the Sophia teachings in the West, and her first great work, *Isis Unveiled*, began the unveiling of the mysteries of the Divine Feminine. In her next great work, *The Secret Doctrine*, Blavatsky elucidates a central teaching of Theosophy, describing the vast unfolding of evolution through seven great globes or epochs of existence.

This teaching of spiritual evolution was elaborated upon by Rudolf Steiner, who gave an even more comprehensive perspective of the unfolding of evolution than Blavatsky. I would like to focus on

Steiner's cosmological perspective as it relates to the Sophia teachings and can deepen our understanding of the mysteries of the Divine Feminine.

Rudolf Steiner was born in Austria in 1861, grew up there, and was educated at the technical high school in Vienna. He received an education in science that later equipped him to become the editor of Goethe's scientific writings. Rudolf Steiner's own early works were of a philosophical nature as he was concerned with epistemology, the theory of knowledge. "How do we come to know things?" was Steiner's central question, and in his primary philosophical work, the *Philosophy of Freedom,* he applied the theory of knowledge to the concept of freedom. He wanted to explore the question "To what extent is the human being a free being?"

Around 1899, Rudolf Steiner had a profound experience that he describes in his autobiography as an encounter with Christ through the Mystery of Golgotha. This experience caused a radical transformation in Rudolf Steiner's inner life and equipped him to become a spiritual teacher. Shortly after this experience he began in 1900 to hold lectures on spiritual themes.

In 1902, Steiner became the general secretary of the Theosophical Society in Germany. He was recognized and acknowledged by Annie Besant, at that time head of the Theosophical Society, as an advanced initiate who was capable of bringing new esoteric teachings into the Theosophical Society. From the outset, Steiner made it clear that he would only be able to fulfill his task if he had complete freedom to include his own esoteric teachings, which he said were appropriate for Western humanity and which had a solid foundation in the Western scientific tradition. Steiner called his approach spiritual science, and saw his teaching as an extension of science as we know it, an extension from focussing on purely material matters to a concern with other dimensions of existence. Steiner's great contribution is that he was able to describe these other levels of existence clairvoyantly and to delineate the human being's relationship to them in a spiritually scientific way.

Steiner remained general secretary of the Theosophical Society in Germany until the end of the year 1912, at which point differences arose which caused Steiner to withdraw from the Society. However, most of the German section of the Theosophical Society remained loyal to him, and he founded a new society, based on spiritual science, called the Anthroposophical Society. Again, with this word *Anthroposophia*, we see a relationship to the Divine Sophia. *Anthropos* is the Greek word for the human being, *Sophia* the word for wisdom. From that time on, Steiner's teaching of spiritual science was renamed Anthroposophy.

Central to Rudolf Steiner's work is his elaboration of Blavatsky's teaching about the seven globes or epochs of evolution. Rudolf Steiner had an extraordinary gift of clairvoyance, and through this gift he was able not merely to theorize, but actually to behold and follow the stages of Earth's evolution into the far distant past. He described four incarnations of the Earth, four incarnations of the Divine Mother, and he showed the evolution of humanity in relation to these incarnations.

The first incarnation or stage of evolution of the Divine Mother Steiner called the Ancient Saturn stage. In cosmological terms, this stage of evolution had no physical manifestation. It was a purely spiritual form of existence, what Steiner called a warmth or a fire stage of evolution. A fiery globe filled the whole solar system extending as far as the orbit of the planet Saturn. So we can conceive of this fiery globe of the Divine Mother as a great womb in which we ourselves existed, together with other spiritual beings. The seeds of the human physical body were formed during this primary stage of evolution.

After a vast period of time, a contraction or dissolution took place, what in the Indian tradition is called *pralaya*. Just as the universe breathes out, so to speak, its primordial energy as the created part of existence during manifestation, so during *pralaya* it withdraws that energy back into itself. During this period after dissolution of the Ancient Saturn globe of warmth, a new globe was formed, but this time it consisted of light and air. This second globe or incarnation of the Divine Mother resembled the Sun in that it was permeated with light and air. This second globe or second incarnation of the Divine Mother, called the Ancient Sun, may be conceived of as a vastly expanded condition of light and air extending up to the orbit of the present planet Jupiter. This second incarnation of the Divine Mother Steiner calls the Ancient Sun stage of evolution, during which human beings received an infusion of life that signified the development of what we can call the life body or the etheric body, which subtly permeates our physical body.

Again, at the end of the Ancient Sun stage of evolution, there was another period of transition or *pralaya* preceding a third incarnation of the Divine Mother. This third stage of evolution signified a further contraction, and the arising of a new cosmic condition as a globe of a watery nature permeated by resounding tones. This third incarnation of the Divine Mother is known as the Ancient Moon stage of evolution, and filled the entire solar system as far as the orbit of the present planet Mars. There was, therefore, a gradual densification from the Ancient Saturn fire stage, to the Ancient Sun stage of air and light, to the Ancient Moon stage of water and sound. As human beings we existed within the womb of the Divine Mother during each of her incarnations. During the Ancient Saturn stage, we received the seed of the physical body; during the Ancient Sun stage, we received the foundation of the etheric or lifebody; and during the Ancient Moon stage of evolution, we received the foundation of the astral body that endowed us with a sentient nature.

Again, at the end of the Ancient Moon stage of evolution, there was a further *pralaya* or period of dissolution, preceding the fourth incarnation of the Divine Mother as our familiar planet Earth. During the present stage of evolution on the Earth, humanity has acquired a fourth level of being, the self or the divine ego, which is endowed with self-consciousness. Every human being is thus a fourfold being, comprising a physical body, etheric body, astral body, and self or divine ego, developed during the Saturn, Sun, Moon, and Earth stages.

Having passed through these four incarnations of Earth with the Divine Mother, how can we envision the further unfolding of evolution? As expressed in the *Our Mother* prayer, now is the time to become awakened to an awareness of our true relationship with the Divine Mother. How can we understand this relationship more deeply? If we look at so-called primitive peoples, such as the Aborigines or the natives of some tribes of South America, they manifest a form of consciousness in which there is still a feeling of unity or oneness with Nature, with the Divine Mother. During the coming of age of humanity in the West, we have more and more emancipated ourselves from our Divine Mother. We have become free and independent beings. But this has been at the expense of losing our deeper relationship with the Earth Mother, forgetting her, as is expressed in the *Our Mother* prayer. Now is the time to remember and renew our relationship with the Divine Mother.

Our relationship to the Divine Mother was very clear to human beings in ancient times and was cultivated in the different mystery centers of antiquity, as at Eleusis, as already mentioned, where the mysteries of Demeter were celebrated. Every human being receiving initiation at Eleusis was able to experience a profound sense of feeling united with Demeter, the Earth Mother. This was the meaning and the gift of the ancient mysteries. At Eleusis, the mysteries were celebrated by worshiping Demeter the mother and Persephone the daughter. Eleusis was close to Athens and so Athena, the patron goddess of the city of Athens, could also be included, in which case we have an expression of the Divine Feminine Trinity of Mother, Daughter, and Holy Soul, with Athena representing the Holy Soul.

As described earlier, with the birth of Christ as the Logos, the mysteries of the Divine Feminine receded into the background. In that moment—through Christ's sacrifice on Golgotha—the development of our divine ego consciousness began, what we have called the coming-of-age of humanity, and this development has continued up until the present time. But now is the time to renew our connection with the Divine Mother. Through a spiritual awakening of humanity to the Divine Feminine, a turning point in spiritual evolution is coming that will signify the beginning of a transformation and spiritualization of the whole Earth.

The completion of this transformation will signify the end of the period of Earth evolution. After another period of transition or *pralaya*, a new globe of existence will emerge that Steiner called Future Jupiter, which will signify a further contraction from our present Earth to the orbit of the planet Venus. This will transform

Earth and humankind into a spiritual state that is described in the Book of Revelation as the Heavenly Jerusalem, the Holy City of the future. The goal of humanity is to reach ever more advanced levels of existence, and during the Future Jupiter period of evolution, or the fifth incarnation of the Divine Mother, the principle of Manas will be developed. *Manas* is a theosophical term and signifies becoming filled with wisdom. The corresponding Western term would be spirit-self or higher self, that is a level of self-consciousness where we become aware of ourselves as spiritual beings united with the whole cosmos. What is conveyed by the word *Manas* is the transformation and spiritualization of the astral body to become elevated to a spirit self.

The period of *pralaya* at the end of the Future Jupiter stage of evolution will be followed by a sixth incarnation of the Divine Mother signifying a still further stage of spiritualization of the Earth and humanity. This period of evolution is called Future Venus and will arise through a further condensation or contraction that will take place as a sixth globe in the place of the orbit of the planet Mercury. This future stage of evolution will signify a spiritualization not just of the astral body, but also of the life body, the etheric body, which will become a radiant healing body. The theosophical term *Buddhi* describes this healing body, what we in the West would term a life-spirit body. We can catch a glimpse of the extraordinary transformation of the life body into a radiant healing body if we look at the example of Jesus healing people through his mere presence. Jesus Christ represents a very advanced stage of evolution at which we will arrive, generally speaking, in the far distant future through intense spiritual work upon ourselves. The whole of nature, which is permeated with life forces, will also become transformed through this work, and eventually humanity together with the Earth will ascend to a still higher spiritual level of existence.

The seventh globe, the goal of all evolution, leads toward the future planetary condition called Vulcan, and it will follow the Future Jupiter and Future Venus stages of evolution. In the Vulcan level of evolution, the Earth will become a Sun located in the present position of the Sun at the center of our solar system. The ultimate goal of spiritual evolution from now into the future will signify the transformation of the Earth into that Sun. At the same time human beings will experience a profound transformation such that the physical body itself will become transformed into a radiant spiritual vehicle, or resurrection body. Jesus attained such a body at his Resurrection, and this gives us a glimpse of the Future Vulcan stage of evolution. As described in the Gospel of St. John, in his resurrection body Jesus Christ was able pass through closed doors, to eat with his disciples, and to materialize or de-materialize the physical body at will. This signifies that he had complete command over his physical body. This is the ultimate goal of evolution in the seventh incarnation of the Divine Mother. At this stage the Divine Mother will become reunited with the Divine Father, for the Divine Mother—as expressed in the *Our Mother* prayer—is eternally faithful to the Divine Father through all cycles of time.

To summarize this cosmological perspective of evolution, we can speak of a primordial stage of evolution when the Father and the Mother were united. But with the beginning of the creation at the start of the Ancient Saturn stage of evolution there began a separation between the Father and the Mother, a separation that gradually increased with each succeeding stage of evolution. At the present Earth stage of evolution we are experiencing the most profound degree of separation between the Divine Father and the Divine Mother. But through the Mystery of Golgotha and Christ's descent into the Earth to unite with the Divine Mother, we have the beginning of a long process of spiritualization of the Earth and humanity that will culminate in the union or the re-integration of the Divine Mother and the Divine Father.

From this perspective, we can see that the great plan of evolution confirms Sophia's words from the Book of Proverbs: *Wisdom has built her house, she has set up her seven pillars.* The seven stages of evolution are the seven pillars in the temple of Sophia. They constitute the architecture of the temple of evolution. It was Rudolf Steiner's great contribution to have unveiled this plan of the divine architecture of evolution.

Of course, in putting forward this extraordinary cosmological perspective of evolution, Rudolf Steiner defies the Darwinian theory of a purely material development. It may be difficult for modern human beings, educated in the light of Darwin's theory, to understand or accept the vision of spiritual evolution that is presented to us by Rudolf Steiner. How, therefore, can we begin to grasp this new perspective? As with many spiritual teachings, understanding it involves meditating upon it, contemplating it, and trying to discover within oneself whether it resonates with what one has already understood of existence. The beautiful thing about Steiner's description is that it shows there is a unity between human evolution and cosmic evolution. When we can begin to grasp that we ourselves are bound up with the planet Earth, that we ourselves have gone through these stages of incarnation of the Earth, that at each stage we ourselves have entered into a higher level of consciousness, then our very existence begins to take on a higher meaning and significance. From the standpoint of the Sophia teachings, both Blavatsky and Steiner each in their own way, with the founding of Theosophy and Anthroposophy, were bearers of the message of this New Age of the Divine Feminine that is in the process of awakening.

Chapter Seven
Reincarnation and the Second Coming

T HE RUSSIAN POET AND PHILOSOPHER, VLADIMIR
Solovyev, wrote many beautiful and inspiring poems based
on his visions of Sophia. Here is one from the year 1898:

*Between waking and dreaming, at all times you are there, day
and night.*
*Your gaze penetrates me to my innermost core, full of radiance,
full of strength. The ice melts. Billowing clouds dissolve into
light.*
Flowers are blooming all around me.
Transparent tones sound silently in the ethers.
*Everywhere I sense you. All around only water and light, and in
the blue shimmering distance the All flows to me in unity. Yet
the eyes remain, radiant like stars, in the flight of all appearance.*

This wonderful poem evokes for us something of the mystical experience of the Divine Sophia. Perhaps in the ancient mystery temples of Egypt the priests of the mysteries experienced Divine Isis in much the same way, entering into communion with her whose being resounded tone, beauty, light, warmth, and grace. We are now living in the New Age, when the possibility of such experiences is opening up again for all human beings. This raises the question of what the New Age is. I believe that it is an essential part of the Sophia teachings to understand the New Age and the role of the Divine Feminine in this New Age.

If we look to H. P. Blavatsky, Rudolf Steiner, and Valentin Tomberg as heralds of the New Age, a common element in their teaching is the idea of reincarnation. This, too, belongs to the unfolding mysteries of the Divine Feminine. Every human being needs to understand and experience that they have lived on Earth in previous physical bodies, or incarnations, and that our present life can really only be understood on a deeper level as a continuation, a consequence, a metamorphosis of those previous lives. Madame Blavatsky and Rudolf Steiner shared a common goal in bringing the teaching of reincarnation to Western humanity. The whole panorama of cosmic evolution as described by Rudolf Steiner only makes sense against the background of reincarnation. Of course, in the oriental traditions of Hinduism and Buddhism reincarnation has been taught as a matter of fact for thousands of years.

We might, therefore, wonder: Why was the idea of reincarnation excluded in the West? For example, why did Jesus not teach reincarnation? To understand this question, we need to grasp that Western humanity had to pass through a particular period of time not knowing about reincarnation and karma, in order to develop the sense of being a free and independent personality. We can see how knowledge of reincarnation and its consequences, namely the idea of karma or destiny, could prevent someone from unfolding their free initiative. How may we understand this? If we look at the Hindu culture, where reincarnation and karma have always been taught, we can see that there has been a tendency to develop a certain passivity in relationship to life. That is, there is the danger of becoming a fatalist, of having the feeling that life is predetermined by fate, according to one's karma or destiny, and that therefore one is really powerless to affect or influence one's life. Of course, this is a superficial understanding of reincarnation and karma. On a more advanced level, we also find in Hinduism and in Buddhism the concept of overcoming and transforming one's destiny. Nevertheless, in the wise guidance and unfolding of evolution, it was necessary for Western humanity to be oblivious to the idea of reincarnation and karma, at least for a period of time. That has been the case during the last two thousand years.

If we look at Christianity, we find no indication of reincarnation except for one statement by Jesus in the Gospel of St. Matthew, where he points to John the Baptist as being the reincarnated prophet Elijah: *Among those born of women there has arisen no one greater than John the Baptist....And if you are willing to accept it, he is Elijah.* Early in the last century, Rudolf Steiner also spoke of Elijah reincarnating as John the Baptist. This is the only example we can find in the Gospels that points specifically to reincarnation. But, as Jesus himself said to his disciples: *There are many things that I cannot teach you now but which you will understand later and which will be shown to you by the spirit of truth, the Holy Spirit.* With these words, Christ is really pointing to a later age when the idea of reincarnation would become accessible even within a Christian context. We understand reincarnation as one of the teachings that Christ could not bring to Western humanity two thousand years ago, but which is to come forward again now in this New Age.

So what is the New Age? There are many different ideas about it, one of the most widespread being that the New Age is the Age of Aquarius. However, as any astronomer can confirm, the vernal point, which is the marker of the different astronomical ages, is still in the constellation of Pisces. Therefore, we are at present still in the Age of Pisces. However, the vernal point is moving gradually backwards through Pisces. At the present moment in time the vernal point is at five degrees of Pisces and moving backwards at a rate of one degree every seventy-two years. Thus, we can say that in approximately 2375 CE the vernal point will enter Aquarius, and the Aquarian Age will officially begin. At the present time we are not yet in the Age of Aquarius. Currently, we are at the end of the Age of Pisces, and in a period of transition to the Age of Aquarius, a period prophesied to be full of disturbances on Earth and culminating in the Second Coming of Christ.

When asked by his disciples what would be the signs of his Second Coming, Jesus spoke of war, earthquake, famine, and also signs in the heavens. And if we look at the twentieth century, we can see the evidence of war, earthquake, and famine on an unprecedented scale. For example, the most powerful earthquake ever to rock the North American continent took place in 1906 in San Francisco. An earthquake in Tokyo in 1923 resulted in the death of over one hundred thousand people, and a devastating earthquake hit India in 2001 resulting in another one hundred thousand deaths. And there have been many other earthquakes all over the world. The twentieth century also reveals itself as an unprecedented age of war. In 1914 the First World War broke out, followed by the Second World War in 1939. It is estimated that in the twentieth century alone over one hundred million people have died as a result of war. Again, looking at the problem of famine in different regions of the world, this century provides us with evidence of the death of millions of people due to hunger. Looking at the evidence, the twentieth century seems to fulfill at least some of the criteria mentioned by Christ as presaging his Second Coming.

If the twenty-first century *is* the age of Christ's Second Coming, how can we understand it? I have worked with this question for many years, and have discovered a very interesting time cycle with the help of Anne Catherine Emmerich's visions, a cycle that is connected with Christ's life in an unusual way. From his birth in Bethlehem through the Mystery of Golgotha, Christ lived exactly thirty-three and one-third years. This is a key cycle for understanding the unfolding of the New Age in relation to the Second Coming of Christ. Before going into any details as to the significance of this thirty-three and one-third year cycle, I would just like to draw attention to the fact that the Second Coming of Christ is not to be understood as a return of Christ in a physical body. This would be a complete misunderstanding. The Greek word relating to the Second Coming is *parousia,* which means *presence.* Christ is not speaking of an incarnation, but of a renewed *presence.* We can, therefore, understand Christ's Second Coming as a guiding, inspiring, and transforming *presence* within the Earth's biosphere, that which is known esoterically as the etheric sphere of existence. The etheric sheath could also be described as the aura of Earth; it permeates all the forces of nature, and all forms of life upon the planet. It is in this etheric realm that the presence of Christ may be experienced in the New Age.

Two thousand years ago Christ incarnated into the physical body of Jesus of Nazareth. The actual descent of Christ into the physical vessel provided by Jesus of Nazareth took place at the Baptism in the Jordan. As it says in the Gospel of St. Luke, the Baptism in the Jordan took place when Jesus was about thirty years old. In actual fact he was twenty-nine years and nine months of age. This incarnation of the divine, cosmic, spiritual being of Christ into the body of Jesus created what Solovyev calls the God-Man, the perfect union of a divine being and a human being. Jesus Christ became the God-Man. Christ in-dwelt this physical body of Jesus of Nazareth for three and one-half years, fulfilling his mission and destiny until his death at Golgotha and the resurrection one and one-half days later. His ministry constitutes the three and one-half culminating years of the thirty-three and one-third year life of Christ. This cycle is a key that unlocks many doors in our present age.

Two thousand years ago Christ incarnated into a male form. His disciples were male, and he proclaimed his teaching in the context of a patriarchal culture, the Jewish culture. Today, with the return of Christ in the etheric realm or biosphere of the Earth, something completely different is taking place. The etheric body is invisible to physical sight, but clairvoyants can see it subtly permeating the physical body, and maintaining its flow of life energy. The Second Coming is taking place in the etheric realm of existence.

In order to grasp the full significance of this we need to ponder a fundamental esoteric fact. That is, every man has a female etheric body, and every woman has a male etheric body. The implication, therefore, of Christ's return in an etheric body is that the Divine

Feminine is being activated. It is a polarity to the Divine Masculine that was activated by Christ two thousand years ago.

Evidence of the ushering-in of the Age of the Divine Feminine can be found in the work of Valentin Tomberg, and specifically in the *Our Mother* prayer taught by him. I believe this is the central prayer for the new dispensation of Christ now taking place, just as two thousand years ago the central prayer of Christianity was the *Our Father*, the *Lord's Prayer*. With the return of Christ in the etheric realm, it is the *Our Mother* prayer that Christ himself is teaching, and it was given by Christ, through Valentin Tomberg, to humanity. This great prayer, the *Our Mother*, reveals the significance of the Second Coming of Christ. Just as two thousand years ago Christ's mission was the salvation of humanity, now, with the return of Christ in the etheric, he is coming for the redemption of the Earth, and all Earth's beings. Now is the time for the spiritual transformation of the planet.

The *Our Mother* prayer conveys to us that we have a unique role to play in helping the work of Christ in the transformation, spiritualization, and redemption of our Divine Mother Earth. This is the profound meaning of the New Age, so we can see how important it is that we grasp the reality, the livingness of the Divine Feminine, and learn to see the whole planet as a living being. Some astronauts who have looked down upon the Earth from outer space have shared that it seems a most beautiful, blue-shrouded planet, and that it has a truly extraordinary feminine appearance, like a jewel in cosmic space radiating goodness. Astronauts have described the immense feeling of love and unity that they have felt for Mother Earth. Something of this feeling can now be awakened in each one of us, without our having to go out into outer space, if we turn our inner hearts and minds to the Christ, and to his work now in the transformation of the whole world of Nature.

The central mystery of the twenty-first century is the mystery of the return of Christ in the etheric realm, and Rudolf Steiner was one of the first to speak of this event. From the year 1910 on, Steiner began to proclaim this return of Christ in the etheric, saying that it was imminent, that it would begin to be noticeable in the 1930s. In fact, for Steiner, this was the greatest spiritual event of the twentieth century, and he saw his whole life's work as a preparation for it. Valentin Tomberg continued this impulse through his teaching of the *Our Mother* prayer and the *Little Rosary*, which help us to grasp and experience this unfolding of the Divine Feminine that is becoming activated now through the Second Coming of Christ.

The Second Coming

Let us now go into more detail concerning the Second Coming. We are not talking here of an instantaneous event, but of something that began gradually unfolding in the twentieth century and that will last for some 2,500 years from 1899 to 4399. There is some overlap here with the Age of Aquarius, which will last around 2,160 years, from 2375 to 4535. During this time, Christ's presence within the etheric aura of the Earth will provide a stimulus for the transformation of the entire planet, and every human being is invited to participate in this work. Solovyev spoke of the human being as the messiah of the cosmos. The German romantic poet Novalis, who was profoundly inspired by Divine Sophia, also spoke of the human being as the messiah of nature. In his view, the beings of nature look toward the human being as a potential messiah for their kingdom, just as we look to Christ as a messiah for humanity. This signifies that we human beings have a task, a mission, and a responsibility to help in the work of the spiritualization and transformation of nature. Humanity's responsibility toward nature has by and large been ignored within the history of Christianity up until now. In this respect, the full impact of one of St. Paul's letters to the Romans has not really been grasped by humanity even now. These words of St. Paul refer to the creation eagerly awaiting redemption by the sons and daughters of light:

The whole of creation has been groaning in travail, awaiting redemption through the sons and daughters of light, that she may be freed from the bondage of decay, and may attain the glorious liberty of the children of God.

This groaning in travail refers to the groaning of the beings of nature, looking to humanity for redemption. As an example, we can see how Christ was able to relate to the forces of nature when we recall him stilling the storm on the Sea of Galilee. Jesus was with his disciples in a boat and while he was asleep a great storm suddenly blew up. The disciples, becoming fearful and anxious, awoke him and he arose and spoke to the wind and the waves until they were stilled. The disciples said: *What kind of man is this, that even the wind and the waves obey him?* Why did they obey him? Because they knew the voice of divine love was speaking to them. This is what the beings of nature long to hear, the voice of divine love speaking to them. With the help of Christ, humanity's task is to begin to pour our love, our devotion, our inner warmth, and strength of spirit into the world of nature, to give back to nature what nature has freely bestowed upon us to sustain our very existence.

117

There are examples of saints who have developed something of this quality of love for nature, such as St. Francis of Assisi, who could speak to the birds, and tamed a wild wolf.

> *The fierce wolf came running toward St. Francis and his companions with its mouth open. The saint made the sign of the cross toward it. And the power of God checked the wolf, and made it slow down and close its cruel mouth.*
>
> *Then calling to it, St. Francis said: "Come to me, Brother Wolf. In the name of Christ, I order you not to hurt me or anyone." It is marvelous to relate that as soon as he had made the sign of the cross, the wolf closed its terrible jaws and stopped running. As soon as he gave it that order, it lowered its head and lay down at the saint's feet, as though it had become a lamb.*

The beings of nature could hear and respond to his words of love, which find expression in a most beautiful way in St. Francis' *Hymn to the Sun*, his hymn to the creation, where he speaks of Brother Sun and Sister Moon. This great hymn is a true representation of the new impulse of Sophianic Christianity in the New Age, a Christianity that embodies the impulse of the Divine Feminine, takes account of Mother Nature, and looks to Divine Sophia as the world soul who fills the entire cosmos. This perspective is now being revealed in this New Age of Christianity.

There is, of course, the question: If we cannot see Christ, how can we learn to find him? How is the Christ to be found within the etheric realm? What time cycles underlie his activity? In order to answer these questions, let us return once again to the thirty-three and one-third year cycle, which is a key to understanding the impulse of the New Age.

So when did the New Age begin? As far as I know, Rudolf Steiner was the first person to refer to the New Age, and he pinpointed its beginning to the year 1899. This was the same year in which he had the profound, mystical experience of Christ that transformed his whole life and awakened him to become a prophet of the etheric Christ. According to Rudolf Steiner, the year 1899 was the last year of Kali Yuga, what in the Hindu tradition is called the Age of Darkness. Kali Yuga extended over a five thousand year period beginning in February 3102 BCE. Five thousand years later brings us to the year 1899, when, therefore, the next yuga, the Satya Yuga began. In Hindu terminology this means the Age of Light. In 1899, therefore, there began the Age of Light. The word *satya* means truth. We can understand the Age of Light, therefore, to be an age of the light of truth beginning to shine upon us. What stands behind this shining in of the light of truth? It is the return of Christ radiating his etheric presence for the benefit of the whole planet.

According to Steiner's understanding of the Hindu yugas, each age lasts half as long as the preceding one. So the Satya Yuga that began in 1899 will last 2,500 years, this being half the length of the five thousand-year period of the preceding Kali Yuga. The New Age will extend from 1899 to the year 4399, at which time the etheric Christ will withdraw from the biosphere of Earth, and then will begin to work on the astral plane of existence.

We can see that Christ works from age to age to guide the unfolding of human evolution. Two thousand years ago he addressed humanity on the physical level of existence, but now he is addressing humanity from the etheric or life level of existence, and in 2,500 years' time he will begin to address humanity from the astral, or soul level of existence. Then again, in a still further distant era of time, he will address humanity from the egoic or *devachanic* level of existence, the spiritual level of existence. Thus, we see how Christ leads humanity on Earth from stage to stage, ever higher, in this unfolding course of evolution.

Rudolf Steiner links the New Age with this event of the Second Coming of Christ. He explains that the thirty-three and one-third year cycle, the length of Christ's life, is of key significance. How can we grasp this? During the life of a normal human being the etheric body is united with the physical body between birth and death, and only separates from it at the moment of death, leaving the physical body behind as a corpse. All the experiences of our life are imprinted into the etheric body. At the moment of death, when the etheric body is released from the physical body, a series of flashbacks, or images, detailing our whole life, emerges in a majestic panorama. Many people who have had near-death experiences have beheld this extraordinary tableau. In the case of a normal human being, the etheric body begins to dissolve back into the etheric cosmos at the moment of death. This usually takes about three days. In the case of the Christ, who had completely spiritualized his etheric body, there was no dissolution of this etheric body at the moment of his death or resurrection. So Christ was able to dwell within his etheric body, and it was in this etheric body that the Ascension of Christ took place forty days after the Resurrection. As Christ himself said, when he spoke to Mary Magdalene in the Garden of Gethsemane on Easter Sunday morning: *Do not touch me, for I have not yet ascended to my Father, but go and tell the disciples that I will ascend to the Father in heaven.* With these words, Christ was proclaiming that his ascent in his etheric body to the realm of the Father would begin forty days later.

In the Christian esoteric tradition, the millions upon millions of stars shining in the heavens can be understood as an outer manifestation of the realm of the Father. As Jesus said: *In my Father's house are many mansions.* The fixed stars of the zodiac are considered the central belt in this whole world of stars, and after death the soul ascends through the succeeding planetary realms of the Moon, Mercury, Venus, the Sun, Mars, Jupiter, Saturn, to enter this world of the fixed stars. This journey of the soul after death is described in Dante's great work the *Divine Comedy*. Rudolf Steiner also chronicled this journey of the soul after death.

Every human being makes this journey after death, and eventually enters the world of the fixed stars. There the decision is made to re-incarnate upon the Earth. At the moment of making this decision, consideration is made for the needs of a new physical body. The human being then engages in the activity of building up the archetype of the physical body from the constellations of the fixed stars, drawing the forces needed for the head from the constellation of Aries, the forces needed for the larynx from the constellation of Taurus, for the shoulders and arms from the constellation of Gemini, and so on down, drawing the forces for the feet from the constellation of Pisces. The spirit seed, the archetype of the physical body, is built up containing the forces of all the constellations of the zodiac. The soul then begins the descent through the planetary spheres in reverse order, returning with this spirit seed, the archetype for the physical body, and eventually entering into the sphere of the Moon. It is here that the event of conception takes place, where the egg is fertilized in the womb of the mother. At approximately this moment, the incarnating soul sends down the spirit seed to unite with the fertilized egg in the mother's womb, where it becomes active in the building-up of the physical body. We could say, therefore, that our physical body is a cross between that which we have received through heredity from our parents, and that which we have brought down ourselves from the world of the stars. To arrive at an understanding as to how the human being is formed in the image and likeness of the cosmos is essential to the New Age of the emergence of the Divine Feminine. The human soul mirrors the cosmic soul, Sophia. Raising the veil of Sophia or Isis, we gain a glimpse of profound star mysteries. This living wisdom of the stars is inspired by Divine Sophia herself, and will emerge during the course of the New Age. It will entail a living understanding of how the human being reincarnates, how the human being is related to the world of stars, and how, through reincarnation, human karma or destiny is carried over from one life to the next.

The return of Christ follows this same archetype. After his death, Christ ascended in his etheric body through the realms of the planets into the realm of the fixed stars, and now he is returning from this realm of the Father down again through the planetary spheres to Earth. This ascent began on Ascension Day in the year 33 CE, which was the year of his crucifixion and resurrection. Fifty-six revolutions of the thirty-three and one-third year cycle occurred between CE 33 and 1899. The ascent of Christ's etheric body took place through twenty-eight thirty-three and one-third year cycles, followed by its descent through a further twenty-eight thirty-three and one-third year cycles, and culminated with the beginning of the return of Christ in the etheric realm in the year 1899.

The full impact of Christ's return in the etheric only began to be felt, however, around the year 1930, actually in 1929. Consider that the etheric body of the Christ contains all the memories of Christ, and that the most important period in the thirty-three and one-third years of his life is the last three and one-half years, signifying the time between the baptism in the Jordan and the crucifixion and resurrection. It was during these last three and one-half years of his life that Christ began to teach, to perform miracles, and to heal. This culminated with his sacrifice on the Cross, followed by the resurrection. This three and one-half year period is called the ministry of Christ. This means that, although the return of the etheric Christ began in 1899, it was actually some twenty-nine years and ten months later, in the year 1929, that the ministry of the etheric Christ began. (33 1/3 - 3 1/2 = 29 years, 10 months.)

If we look at the course of the twentieth century we see that it is actually shaped by three thirty-three and one-third year cycles that symbolically represent the life of Christ. A true understanding of the unfolding of this thirty-three and one-third year cycle enables us to understand what has been taking place in the twentieth century. We can speak of these three thirty-three and one-third year cycles as stages of the unfolding of the New Age, the Second Coming of Christ, or the New Age of Sophianic Christianity which is inspired by the return of Christ. As we begin to grasp the meaning of his return in the etheric realm, so we understand that Christ's presence (*parousia*) is calling forth the Divine Feminine: that his work is now directed toward the Divine Mother, just as two thousand years ago it was directed toward the Divine Father. The teaching of the three aspects of the Divine Feminine given by Valentin Tomberg—Mother, Daughter, and Holy Soul—is inspired by the new dispensation of the Christ for the New Age.

The Three Thirty-Three and One-Third Year Cycles

Let us now look in closer detail at how these three aspects of the Divine Feminine relate to the thirty-three and one-third year cycle as it unfolded during the course of the twentieth century. In the first thirty-three and one-third year period, the etheric Christ was working on the level of human thinking, unfolding a new life of thought, new spiritual concepts. We can find many of these new spiritual concepts in the work of Rudolf Steiner. He spoke of a New Age understanding of the world, indicating humans to be spiritual beings, and shared his Sophianic perspective on cosmic evolution that we discussed in Chapter Six. Through spiritual science, he opened up many practical applications of spiritual ideas to the realms of education, farming, medicine, art, and religion, as well as therapies for handicapped people. Born in 1861, Rudolf Steiner died in 1925, before the culmination of the first thirty-three and one-third year period of the century in the three and one-half year period between 1929 and 1933. If we ask what was the central impulse of the etheric Christ in this first period culminating between 1929 and 1933, we could say it was to bring to birth in each human being a consciousness of our own divine nature, our own I AM, our own divine ego. As St. Paul says: *Not I but Christ in me.* Therefore, the birth of the divine I AM consciousness is the first step of the New Age.

During the second period, from 1933 to 1966, we see the impulse of the etheric Christ working down from the thinking level into the human life of feeling, the emotional level. The work of the etheric Christ during this period was to create and sow the seeds of spiritual community as reflected in the words: *Where two or three are gathered together in my name, there am I in the midst of them.* This impulse culminated very strongly in the 1960s, when we saw the longing and search for community in many parts of the world, especially in America and Europe.

The third thirty-three and one-third year period extends from 1966 until 1999, culminating in the three and one-half year period from February 1996 through to September 1999. This period signified the activity of the etheric Christ moving down from the feeling life to the level of the human will. It is through the life of the will that we are connected with the whole being of Mother Earth, and a fruit of this new activity of Christ is the awakening of human beings more and more to the idea and experience of the Earth as a living being. Connection with the Earth as a living being can be found in the goddess movement that began in the 1970s, and to a certain extent also in the ecological movement. This ideal is coming to expression in many seekers in the Western world. To characterize this activity of the etheric Christ at the end of the twentieth century, we could speak of an infusion of his life force such that an awakening is taking place in the whole of nature. We can look upon the activity of the etheric Christ as inviting us to rediscover the Earth Mother, Demeter. And we can look upon the etheric Christ as the high priest of the new mysteries of Eleusis in our time.

Two thousand years ago, when the disciples of Jesus asked him what signs would presage his return, he said there would be signs in the heavens. There have indeed been signs in the heavens in the twentieth century. In the year 1996, the comet Hayakutake came into the vicinity of the Earth's orbit exactly at the beginning of this three and one-half year period at the culmination of the twentieth century, the period of the etheric Christ's activity on the level of the will. The comet Hayakutake appeared totally unexpectedly in February 1996 to proclaim the beginning of this significant period. Exactly one year after Hayakutake, the comet Hale-Bopp proclaimed the beginning of the second year of the ministry of the etheric Christ at the end of the twentieth century. For those wishing to understand the message of the comets, Hayakutake and Hale-Bopp speak to us of an extraordinary challenge facing humanity. The orbits of these two comets formed a cross in the heavens, and the crossing-point of the trajectories of these two comets was none other than at the star Algol, in the head of Medusa!

The star Algol has periods of brightness and darkness, and in antiquity, on account of this variability, it was looked upon as the "evil eye" in the head of Medusa. We have already discussed the myth of Perseus and Medusa. Let us return to this myth in order to understand the message of the comets for our time. The evil eye of Medusa, in Greek mythology, was the evil eye of ancient clairvoyance turned against the development of the free human personality. Perseus, the representative of the new power of Greek independent thinking, used his intelligence to overcome Medusa. So if the comets are pointing to Medusa in our time, how can we interpret their message? As we have seen, for modern humanity the evil eye of Medusa is the hypnotizing television screen, or the computer screen, which hypnotizes humans into mechanical thinking and, in the view of mythology, turns them to stone. So the comets Hayakutake and Hale-Bopp are pointing to this challenge, this threat facing modern humanity. In our time, due to overuse of the computer, human thinking has reached a point where it is in danger of becoming mechanized. If this were to continue, it would signify an impasse for the future development of the human being. The way forward is to overcome mechanical thinking by developing a new clairvoyance, what we might call an etheric clairvoyance. Through this new power of clairvoyance we will be able to see into the realm of the life forces, the biosphere of the Earth, and to behold the etheric Christ. The positive message of the comets, therefore, is to stir a transformation of our thinking such that it becomes a power of vision with which we can begin to see into the unseen realm of the life forces. Whether we call these life forces *prana* or *chi*, the etheric, or streams of energy, the promise for the future is to see the flow of these forces within the human body and all around us in the world of nature, and through this to begin to behold the work of the etheric Christ as a radiant sun infusing the world with new forces of divine life.

I realize that comets often have negative connotations. In fact, some observers had a completely false and materialistic interpretation of them. This is highly regrettable. I see the majority of comets in an entirely positive light, as bearers of divine love and wisdom. We need only consider that the comet Hale-Bopp crossed the path of Hayakutake at the star Algol *exactly* on the same day, April 10, as Hayakutake had reached this point one year before. That the paths of the two comets should cross is not unusual. Of course they would form a crossing-point somewhere. But that they should cross at that point exactly on the same day, exactly one year apart, is a sign to us that it is more than mere coincidence. The probability of that being a random occurrence is very remote. So, when we look up to the comets and begin to read what they are saying to us, they point to a vast cosmic intelligence, a higher wisdom and power of divine love that speaks to us from the world of stars. This is all part of Sophia's new revelation. We simply have to learn to read the signs in the heavens in the right way. It is our challenge to begin to awaken, to open our hearts and minds, to this stream of divine love and divine light that the comets have conveyed to us. The comets are signs in the heavens announcing this new activity of the etheric Christ in his work of the redemption of Divine Mother Earth.

We can now begin to understand something of the challenges of the new century. Two thousand years ago, the mystery of Christ was revealed against the background of birth and death. For human beings at that time, death was the great mystery. Through his resurrection, Christ overcame death. In our time, the new mystery we must confront and overcome is the mystery of evil. The unfolding of the new Christ impulse can be seen in the New Age as the drama of the struggle between good and evil. During the twentieth century it was possible to say, literally, that the "gates of hell" had been opened.

Consider, for example, the problem of drugs that threaten so many millions of people. It is a problem of facing demonic beings. Anyone who has worked with drug patients, as I have, is aware that one is battling against something much more than solely a substance such as heroin. One can speak also of the "heroin demon" that takes hold of a human being when they use this substance. This is one area where we must confront and overcome evil.

We experienced a demonic manifestation of evil in the phenomenon of the Nazi movement in Germany before and during the Second World War. Hitler became chancellor in Germany in 1933, which coincides with the culmination of the first thirty-three and one-third year cycle in the twentieth century. Humanity had to deal with the ghastly problem of Nazism that precipitated the Second World War and the slaughter of many millions of innocent people.

To illumine the apocalyptic struggle of our time, which is a drama of the Divine Sophia, I would like to draw attention to the main challenge in each of the thirty-three and one-third year periods of the twentieth century. We can contemplate these challenges in the light of St. John's great vision of Divine Sophia found in Chapter Twelve of the Book of Revelation, where he speaks of the woman clothed with the Sun, with the Moon under her feet, and on her head a crown of twelve stars. Then he states that the woman is being threatened by a dragon. If we ponder this powerful image of the Divine Sophia being threatened by the dragon, we can see how in the course of the Nazi movement in Germany and in Stalinist Russia, the head of the dragon did indeed become a grave threat and caused untold suffering. We cannot ignore this problem of evil. Interestingly, Rudolf Steiner focussed primarily upon bringing the new Sophia revelation to Germany, and Vladimir Solovyev brought the Eastern Sophia teachings to Russia. Perhaps, here, we can see the hand of Divine Sophia at work, since Germany and Russia were then attacked by the forces of darkness that we have symbolized by the dragon.

In 1933, that dragon raised its head from the abyss in the form of a powerful temptation that was presented through Hitler to the world. This was the temptation of the will to power. In the Gospels we find an archetype of the three temptations of Christ in the wilderness. The first temptation is that of the will to power, shown by the devil's offer to give Jesus dominion over all the lands of the world if he will bow down to him. The second temptation relates to human feeling life, where Christ is challenged by the devil to save himself from plunging from the pinnacle of the Temple. The third temptation relates to the human life of thought, shown by Satan's challenge to Jesus to turn stones into bread.

The symbolism of these temptations has significance for our own time. The temptation of the will to power as it came to expression two thousand years ago was that of the tempter appearing to Jesus Christ and saying: *If you bow down and worship me I will give you all the kingdoms of the world.* This was exactly the temptation that Hitler presented first to the German people, but his intention was to become ruler of the whole world. The temptation he presented was: *If you bow down and worship me I will give you everything you need.* Through this temptation of the will to power, there came about the immense struggle against evil in the twelve-year period from 1933 to 1945. Eventually, and against great odds, this power of evil was crushed through the victory of the British and American allies defeating Germany and Japan in the Second World War.

Contemplating the second thirty-three and one-third year cycle from 1933 to 1966, we see a new temptation directed at the human feeling life. This is the temptation where the devil tells Jesus to save himself by way of plunging from the pinnacle of the Temple. What does this mean in an esoteric sense? The pinnacle of the Temple is the height of human consciousness, rational thought, and the power of human conscience. The drug epidemic that began in the 1960s was a temptation to escape from our rational consciousness and to plunge down into our life of instincts. The slogan "Turn on, tune in, drop out," is a modern-day version of the devil's prompting Jesus to cast himself down from the pinnacle of the Temple. We can see in the present-day continuation of the drug problem that we are still dealing with this temptation.

In the 1990s, with increasing strength, the third temptation was directed to human thought life. It is the temptation to substitute the dead for the living, to substitute stones for bread. This means to put in the place of reality something created by artificial means. The words *virtual reality* bring this temptation clearly to expression. Every time we take in artificially created impressions in the belief that they are something more than they really are, we are changing stones into bread, substituting something lifeless in place of the living. The comets Hayakutake and Hale-Bopp drew attention to the temptation of becoming subject to mechanical thinking and, therefore, of being hypnotized by the "evil eye." This is the third temptation of the twentieth century.

The struggle between good and evil, and the powerful image of Sophia as the world soul being attacked by the dragon, show us that what is at stake here is nothing less than the battle for the human soul. The dragon, symbolizing the forces of darkness, desires to take over and dominate the human soul. And just as two thousand years ago Christ lived through these three temptations in the wilderness, now, with the Second Coming of Christ in the etheric realm, the whole of humanity similarly has to live through these three temptations. This is the drama of the twentieth century, and of course these three temptations are continuing now in the new millennium. After Christ triumphed over these temptations two thousand years ago, *angels came and ministered unto him.* In the same way, when we triumph over the three temptations directed to our faculties of thought, feeling, and will, we are promised an opening to the spiritual dimensions of existence, where angels will come and minister to us.

The battle with the forces of darkness is intrinsic to grasping the unfolding of the Divine Feminine in our time. At the end of his life Vladimir Solovyev wrote *A Short Tale of Antichrist*, where he confirmed humanity's challenge to encounter the powers of evil and thereby to awaken to new spiritual levels of consciousness. We need to awaken to the Divine Sophia's heavenly forces, and to help her in the work of the transformation of the Earth, which means coming to terms with evil.

In looking at these three periods of the twentieth century, it seems that in the first thirty-three and one-third year period there was an extraordinary infusion of the light of truth, the light of Divine Sophia, through individuals such as Rudolf Steiner. In the second thirty-three and one-third year period, the third Person of the Feminine Trinity, the Holy Soul, came to expression in the impulse toward spiritual community. And during the last thirty-three and one-third year period, there has been an awakening to the Divine Mother, the first Person of the Divine Feminine Trinity.

Among those who have experienced an awakening to the Divine Mother, it is often the case that there awakens at the same time the understanding that historical Christianity has done much to suppress the mysteries of the Divine Feminine. Very often this knowledge is accompanied by a mood of wanting to turn away from Christianity. This, however, would signify "throwing the baby out with the bath water." For the Christ himself is now actively engaged in the work of redemption of the Divine Mother. We gain a fuller picture of the unfolding of the Divine Feminine in the twentieth century against the background of the *parousia,* the *presence* of the Christ, who is now awakening us to a new face of the Divine.

Valentin Tomberg was dedicated to bringing a new spiritual impulse into the twentieth century in what he called Christian hermeticism. What does Christian hermeticism have to do with the new revelation of the Divine Feminine? In order to understand this, let us look back to the origin of the hermetic tradition. It dates back to Egypt and to the ancient sage Hermes, who was for the Egyptian people what Moses was for the people of Israel. Hermes taught the priests of Egypt the essence of the Egyptian religion. He taught the mysteries, the science of the stars, and of writing in hieroglyphs.

Hermes was one of the great teachers of humanity, who was inspired by Christ and Sophia in their pre-Christian, pre-incarnational form. He taught devotion to Osiris and Isis.

For Hermes, Osiris was the pre-Christian form of Christ, and Isis was the pre-Christian form of Sophia. Osiris and Isis, therefore, are the same beings as those whom we now call Christ and Sophia, the Son and the Daughter. We can conceive of a metamorphosis from the mysteries of Hermes in ancient Egypt to the activity of Christ and Sophia in the etheric realm today. This is a key to understanding Valentin Tomberg's teaching on Christian hermeticism. If we read the seminal work, *Meditations on the Tarot: A Journey into Christian Hermeticism,* we find in this work a fusion of Christianity and the ancient Egyptian hermetic tradition. We also find practical instructions for treading the spiritual path of Christian hermeticism. Finally, we find a new way of relating to these divine beings, Christ and Sophia. Valentin Tomberg shows humanity the possibility of finding a new spiritual relationship with Christ and Divine Sophia.

In the Book of Revelation, Christ is described as the Lamb and Sophia is the Bride of the Lamb. The Book of Revelation points to the coming into existence of a new Heaven and a new Earth through the sacred marriage of the Lamb and his Bride. This wonderful vision that is presented at the end of the Book of Revelation depicts the goal toward which humanity and the Earth is striving as a New Jerusalem. How will the creation of this New Jerusalem come about? In the Book of Revelation, John has a vision where the Bride of the Lamb descends from heavenly realms, bringing the forces of the new heaven with her, while the Lamb is depicted as having sacrificed himself in order to bring about a transformation of the Earth, in which the entire Earth is raised up in spiritualized form. The sacred marriage of the Lamb and his Bride signifies this union of Sophia and Christ, and points us toward the goal of our present Earth—the arising of the New Jerusalem, as the next globe of evolution, or what Steiner calls the future Jupiter stage of evolution.

The creation of a new Heaven and a new Earth signifies the awakening to the Divine Mother and an awakening to Sophia as the World Soul. At the dawn of the new millennium, I see an itensification of Divine Sophia's inflowing energies uniting with Christ's outpouring grace as an opening of the entire planet to become a Grail vessel to receive a new infusion of divine life. This extraordinary infusion will help enliven the whole of nature, and we can participate in it if we are not cut off from nature. This event will signify the calling forth from the depths of the Earth the lost kingdom of Shambhala, the golden realm of the Divine Mother in the heart of the Earth. As a result, more and more human beings will begin to find access to the kingdom of Shambhala: we will begin to feel a paradisiacal quality in our relation to nature and will begin to experience a new connection and unity with the entire planet.

Understanding this message of the Sophia teachings is essential for a true grasp of the start of the New Age in the twentieth century, and of what is to come as the further unfolding of the New Age during the new millennium.

Chapter Eight
Other Traditions

I THINK IT IS POSSIBLE TO PARALLEL THE TEACHING of Sophia in other spiritual traditions, especially those of the East. For example, the Divine Mother is known in Chinese Taoism as the Tao, the mother of all things. Taoism is an ancient spiritual tradition whose goal is to promote an experience of the harmony between heaven and earth, and a feeling of oneness with nature. In the Taoist tradition, it is taught that human beings can experience an essential oneness with nature in the sighing of the wind, in the falling of the rain, in the sounds of rushing water, and other natural phenomena. Something of this experience is becoming accessible now through the reawakening to the Divine Mother that is taking place in our time. The new experience of Shambhala will also be an experience of the harmony of the Tao, and will help to redress the unfortunate imbalance that has arisen between humanity and nature. On a spiritual level this is an answer to the ecological crisis of our time. But it all depends upon whether humanity is open in heart and mind for this new experience. Without some such experience it is easy to see that there will be a dramatic worsening of our ecological crisis.

In order to understand how this experience of unity will impress itself upon us if we begin to attune to the world of nature, many people, including myself, have begun to experience a new sense of vibrancy, a new quality of light within nature. This is one of the characteristics pointing to the awakening that is now taking place upon our planet. One friend of mine described a recent experience where he could see the inpouring of light into nature and the appearance of nature as a great feminine being. As he described it, an image of the goddess Artemis suddenly awoke within him. This and other spiritual experiences point to this reawakening to the Divine Mother. As if to confirm it, interest in the various mystery centers dedicated to the Divine Mother in the ancient world—for example, that of Artemis in Ephesus and that of Demeter in Eleusis—is arising in human consciousness once again.

It is also possible to awaken to the Earth as a living being if one looks upon the different regions of the Earth as organs in the body of the Divine Mother. In this vision, Africa appears as the heart of Mother Earth, the Pacific Ocean as the womb of Mother Earth, and the great mountain chain, extending from Alaska through the Rocky Mountains and the Andes to the tip of South America, appears as the spinal column of Mother Earth, making the regions of these mountains extremely important for the unfolding of the new consciousness of Mother Earth as a living being. Thus, we can also look upon the different countries as embodying different aspects or different organs of the Earth.

Of course, this awakening to the Earth as a living being is not something that we can expect to be reported in the news. It is an individual, mystical experience, but one that more and more people are having. As an orientation toward this experience, I recall a profound meditation on the Divine Mother that was given by Rudolf Steiner. In this meditation the Divine Mother is understood as a living, feeling being who is the spiritual origin of all matter. Here she speaks in her own words to humanity:

If you seek me with true desire for knowledge, I shall be with you.
I am the seed and the source of your visible world.
I am the ocean of light in which your soul lives.
I am the ruler of space.
I am the creator of cycles of time.
Fire, air, light, water, and earth obey me.
Feel me as the spiritual origin of all matter.
And as I have no consort on Earth, call me Maya.

In this last line, we have a reference to the fact that as long as we do not see the Earth as a living being, we are living in Maya, illusion, and that through awakening to the Earth as a living being, we become true companions of the Divine Mother. This meditation points to the Mother as the ruler of space, and the creator of cycles of time: it confirms that we are sustained by the Mother in the ocean of light, and that all the elements of Nature—fire, air, light, water, and earth—obey her. This meditation can guide us to an awakening of the vastness and majesty of the Divine Mother. I recommend meditating upon these words every day and allowing them to become a source of inspiration in our daily lives. As we relate to the universe and to the whole world of nature around us we will begin to experience the being-ness and the I-ness, the individuality or the *person*, if you will, of the Divine Feminine.

To return to the world religions, we also find in Hinduism a clear knowledge of the Divine Mother whose outer aspect manifests itself as Nature or Mother Earth. Sri Aurobindo, who lived from 1872 to 1950, was one of the finest twentieth-century representatives of Hinduism. Here is a quotation from his work, *The Mother:*

> *The universal Mother works out whatever is transmitted by her transcendent consciousness from the Supreme and enters into the worlds that she has made. Her presence fills and supports them with the divine spirit and the divine all-sustaining force and delight without which they could not exist. That which we call nature or prakriti is only her most outward executive aspect.*

Here, Sri Aurobindo exemplifies the ancient Indian tradition of devotion to the Divine Mother as the creative being who sustains us here in our existence upon the Earth. Sri Aurobindo also points to the wisdom aspect of the Divine Feminine in words that remind us of the Sophia texts in the Old Testament. For Sri Aurobindo, the Divine Wisdom is Maheshvari.

> *Maheshvari is seated in the wideness above the thinking mind and will and sublimates and greatens them into wisdom and largeness or floods with a splendor beyond them. For she is the mighty and wise one who opens us to the supramental infinities and cosmic vastness, to the grandeur of the supreme light, to a*

treasure house of miraculous knowledge, to the measureless movement of the Mother's eternal forces. Tranquil is she and wonderful, great and calm for ever. Nothing can move her, because all wisdom is in her.

Another important Indian figure is Ramakrishna (1836–1886), who dedicated his life to worshiping that aspect of the Divine Feminine spoken of in Hinduism as Kali, the consort of Shiva. Also we remember Radha, the consort of Krishna, one of the central deities of the Hindu religion. According to the *Brahma Vavarta Purana*, Radha is the force that leads humanity across samsara, the ocean of the world of change, back to its spiritual home. She represents the holy wisdom of all that exists.

In Buddhism, Prajna corresponds to the Hindu Shakti, or Divine Mother. The hymn to Prajna Paramita is a hymn in praise of the perfect wisdom of Divine Sophia, who manifests in Buddhism as the goddess Tara. Numerous representations of Tara in her various forms are to be found in painting and sculpture. Reading the Hymn to Perfect Wisdom, or the Liturgy of the 108 Names of Holy Tara, we find an astonishing similarity to the description in the Books of Wisdom of the Old Testament referring to Divine Sophia. In fact, the similarity between the texts is almost perplexing. It seems unlikely that any borrowing took place, though if this had been the case the Buddhist Mahayana texts, which appeared later, would have been influenced by the Wisdom Books of the Old Testament. Considering the philosophical differences of the two traditions it is more likely that any apparent similarity is due to a common experience of eternal Wisdom, whether we call her Shakti, Radha, Tara, or Divine Sophia.

In the Buddhist tradition the goddess Tara appears in different
aspects, such as Arya Tara, the noble Tara, who leads seekers over the
sea of *samsara* to the otherworldly shore of *nirvana*. There is also
Sitatapatra Tara, the thousandfold helper, who is depicted as a radiant
white goddess standing on a lotus and surrounded by a halo of flame.
She has compassionate eyes, which gaze upon all the beings of the
different worlds. Then there is the Astamangala Devi, the goddess of
the eight favorable signs, who promises happiness, is rich in content
and yet simple in form, and whose contemplation is meant to effect
a sublime experience of the divine. Astamangala Devi has four heads,
signifying that she watches over all four directions in order to keep
her gaze on those who belong to her. She has a round banner,
indicating that she is the world's axis and apex, the soul and mother
of the universe. Then there is the Syama Tara, the green Tara, who
combines symbols from both Indian and Chinese traditions. She is
seated in a relaxed meditation position, her upper body decorated
with jewels, and her youthful head crowned by a radiant diadem.
Lastly, there is the goddess of mercy, Kwan-Yin, of the Chinese
Buddhist tradition:

> *The men love her, the children adore her, and the women chant
> her prayers. Whatever the temple may be, there is nearly always
> a chapel for Kwan-Yin within its precincts, she lives in many
> homes, and in many, many hearts she sits enshrined....Other
> gods are feared, she is loved....Her countenance is radiant as
> gold, and gentle as the moonbeam; she draws near to the people
> and the people draw near to her. Her throne is upon the isle
> of...Pu T'o...to which she came floating upon a water-lily. She is
> the model of Chinese beauty, and to say that a lady or a little girl*

is a "Kwan-Yin" is the highest compliment that can be paid to grace and loveliness.

All of these representations of the various goddesses from the Hindu and Buddhist traditions point to different aspects of Divine Sophia. Some of the aspects relate more to compassion, the quality of the heart, while the gnostic aspect relates to enlightenment, divine wisdom, and knowledge. Yet another aspect relates more to our will, a third level of manifestation of Divine Sophia. In the world religions of Taoism, Hinduism, and Buddhism, and also in other religions, we find a presence of the Divine Feminine in her various aspects. This universality of Sophia helps us to understand that we can learn from all the different traditions and acquire an ever-deeper love and knowledge and respect for what they convey to us concerning the Divine Feminine.

Within the Christian tradition, as we have seen, Sophia was actually incarnated within the Virgin Mary, and as an indication that the Divine Feminine has intensified her activity in the New Age, consider the many apparitions of the Virgin Mary taking place around the world. I see this as a counterpart to the manifestation of the Christ as a presence in the etheric realm. Most commentators point back to the year 1830, in Paris, as commencing this new sequence of apparitions of the Virgin Mary. Interestingly, her first important appearances all took place in France. In addition to her appearance in Paris, she also appeared in 1846 on a mountain called La Sallette near Grenoble, and in 1858 at Lourdes where she appeared to the young fourteen-year-old Bernadette and pointed to place in a grotto where Bernadette should dig up part of the soil. When Bernadette scooped away the soil, a spring began to issue forth from the spot, and it was conveyed to Bernadette that this spring was of holy water that had healing powers.

In this apparition we see the close relationship between Divine Sophia as the bearer of cosmic wisdom manifesting through the Virgin Mary, and the Divine Mother as the living being of the Earth. The Virgin Mary, as the incarnation of Divine Sophia, was able to point to the healing source of the spring that issued forth from the Earth. Shortly after this miracle, a blind person put the water on his eyes and was healed. And since that time many thousands of people have been healed through the water issuing forth from Lourdes, making this the most visited pilgrimage site of the Virgin Mary in the Western world.

One of the most important twentieth-century manifestations of the Virgin Mary took place at Fatima, a little village in Portugal, in 1917, where she appeared, once a month, over a period of six months, to three peasant children. Her appearances culminated in an extraordinary vision of the Sun as a rotating wheel of colored light that was seen by thousands of people who had journeyed to Fatima. During this sequence of apparitions, Mary warned of a coming great catastrophe in Russia if there was not a change of heart among those people. Unfortunately the message was not heeded, and shortly afterwards the Bolshevik Revolution broke out.

Another significant series of apparitions of the Virgin Mary occurred in Amsterdam, between 1945 and 1959, where she appeared as the Lady of all Nations, or the Lady of all Peoples, and spoke of her new designation as co-redeemer alongside the Christ. There are signs that this prophecy Mary made in Amsterdam may be fulfilled in the not-too-distant future. Yet another series of apparitions that have gained worldwide attention started in 1981, occurring in the little town of Medjugorje in the Bosnian region of Yugoslavia. Again, the Virgin Mary appeared to several young people, in order to convey her message to humanity. The basic message of the Virgin Mary was that we need to awaken, to return to our faith in the Divine; we need to pray; we need to develop qualities of the heart, love our neighbors, and become concerned about what is taking place in the world.

The message of the Virgin Mary here and elsewhere is generally couched in very simple terms, and her appearances are often to children or people without advanced education. Nevertheless, her message is clear: we need to re-awaken to the Divine and return to an active relationship with it. In the meantime, millions of people have visited Medjugorje and have been touched in some way or healed by the Virgin Mary.

Our Lady of Guadalupe
The most famous apparition on the American continent was that of the appearance of Mary in Mexico in 1531 as "Our Lady of Guadalupe." It is due to this apparition that the Virgin Mary is acknowledged as the spiritual patron of America.

The image of Our Lady of Guadalupe shows her standing on a dark crescent Moon amidst the rays of the Sun forming a mandorla (an oval-shaped halo) around her, and her turquoise mantle is studded with golden stars. The likeness of this supernaturally produced image to that of John's vision of Sophia from the Book of Revelation is immediately apparent. Could it be that Our Lady of Guadalupe was a manifestation of *Mary Sophia*, and that it is actually *Mary Sophia* who is the spiritual patron of America?

Our Lady of Guadalupe appeared to an Aztec widower, Juan Diego, who set off on the morning of December 9, 1531, from the

village of Tolpetlac, where he lived, to go to church in the neigh-
boring town of Santiago. When he was passing by the hill called
Tepeyac, he heard the song of many birds singing in wondrous
harmony. He began to climb the hill, which had earlier been the site
of an Aztec temple dedicated to "Our Mother," the goddess
Tonantzin. He saw the top of the hill covered in mist permeated with
colored light, like interpenetrating rainbows. The birds stopped
singing and Juan Diego heard his Aztec name spoken by a woman's
voice. (Juan Diego was his christianized name.) The mist cleared to
reveal a young and beautiful woman in a robe in the colors of Aztec
royalty.

Speaking in Juan Diego's native tongue, the woman asked Juan
Diego where he was going, and he replied that he was going to church
to celebrate a feast day dedicated to the Mother of God. (December
8 is the festival day of the immaculate conception of the Virgin
Mary.) The woman responded by saying that she was the very holy
Virgin Mary, mother of the true God, mother of the creator of heaven
and earth, and that she desired that a temple be built at the foot of
the hill in her honor. She instructed Juan Diego to go to the bishop
to communicate this to him. The Spanish Bishop Zumàrraga, a
Franciscan, listened patiently to Juan Diego's story, and then
requested that he return with a "sign" from the lady as proof that she
really was the Virgin Mary.

Juan Diego returned to the hill of Tepeyac and Mary directed
him to the top of the hill, where he would find the "sign" that would
be proof of her authenticity. Running to the top of the hill, he found
that it had become a garden. To his surprise, on that cold December
morning, he saw red roses blossoming, the rose being a traditional
symbol of Mary (and also of Sophia). These were extraordinary jewel-

like roses, similar to the Castilian roses associated with Spanish royalty. Juan Diego began to gather up the roses in his cactus-fiber tunic or *tilma*, and ran back to the bishop's palace. Finally admitted to see the bishop, he opened his *tilma* and the roses spilled out onto the floor. The bishop and his assistant were visibly struck with awe and wonder, for they beheld on the tunic an imprint of Mary. This was an image of the woman who had appeared to Juan Diego.

This imprint of Mary is visible to this day, for the *tilma* is on display (behind bullet-proof glass) at the shrine—now a basilica—of Our Lady of Guadalupe, not far north of Mexico City. Mary is clothed in a red tunic embroidered with golden symbols, enveloped in a turquoise mantle strewn with golden stars, and surrounded by a mandorla formed by the Sun's rays. She is standing on the Moon. The golden symbol visible at the place of her womb signifies in Aztec, "the heart of the universe." Other Aztec Sun symbols appear on the tunic. Clearly, this image of Mary is not European but is Aztec in origin.

The people to whom Mary Sophia appeared in 1531 were in close connection with the cosmos. The Aztecs honored and appreciated the gifts of the Sun and the rhythms of the Moon. Thus, it is appropriate to associate Our Lady of Guadalupe with Sophia, since she appeared to Juan Diego clothed with the Sun, with the Moon under her feet, and with golden stars adorning her mantle. She appeared as a young, innocent maiden. Speaking poetically, it was in her image that the rose was formed to catch the morning dew, each drop of dew being like a pearl mirroring everything under the Sun, a kind of "nectar of the gods." The maiden's skin was the color of the blush of the roses that Juan Diego found. He discovered the same dewy freshness on the roses that adorned the maiden's youthful appearance like fresh down. This was the same maiden who in her freshness, innocence, and purity carried the child called the "Son of Man." She appeared to Juan Diego "clothed with the Sun," so that he beheld the Spiritual Sun shining forth from her.

Just as Mary gave birth to Jesus two thousand years ago, the Spiritual Sun has now to be born within, to radiate out from each one of us into the world. On the path of spiritual development we are destined to become like rays of the Sun, vivifying and regenerating both the atmosphere around and our own "inner atmosphere." It is interesting that this imprint bestowed by Mary Sophia at her appearance to Juan Diego bears the fullness of the image of Sophia clothed with the raiment of the Sun—the Spiritual Sun or "Christ within." Each one of us is able to connect with this *inner birth process*, absorbing the Spiritual Sun to become permeated with the divine substance of the Sun, analogous to the *physical birth process* that Mary underwent in giving birth to Jesus two thousand years ago.

The morning dew is formed through the meeting of the Earth forces with the warmth of the morning Sun. Similarly, the appearance of Our Lady of Guadalupe was a crystallization from the spirit, like the forming of the morning dew. It was essentially a phenomenon of light and sound, whereby the thoughts of Mary Sophia were transmitted to Juan Diego as if on a beam of light. Such an apparition of Mary enables one to behold Sophia's thinking and to grasp her thoughts toward the Earth and humanity, thoughts proceeding from her radiant heart.

In the being of Mary, who lived and walked the Earth two thousand years ago, there lived an immaculate, pure, unstained heart, like a pure crystal, which was able to directly reflect Divine Sophia. In addition to Mary, we find images of the Divine Feminine in different cultures, all reflecting various aspects of Sophia. These images have been perceived, intuited, felt, and received in imaginations by people throughout the ages, who have endeavored to capture their impressions of the Divine Feminine in art, sculpture, poetry, and writing, etc.

Even though each one of us may feel separate and alone in the "splendid isolation" of our own individuality, we are all offspring of Sophia, the Mother of Humanity. It is possible to become aware of Her and the ever-present aspects of the Divine Feminine which nourish, tend, and guide us on our individual paths. Just as the human eye is able to see by receiving light and forming images, the qualities of the Divine Feminine are inherent in the spiritual light that streams down continually upon us. It is a matter of opening our inner spiritual organs to be able to receive the spiritual light and to form images thereof, just as the physical eyes are able to see and to form images from the light received.

* * *

It is not possible to mention all the recent apparitions of the Virgin Mary. There has been a veritable explosion of these apparitions, all of which point to an intensification of the inflowing Divine Feminine energies during this time of crisis at the end of the twentieth century and the beginning of the twenty-first. The apparitions of the Virgin Mary are an important manifestation of the New Age of the Divine Feminine that is beginning now. Understanding Sophia in the New Age involves envisioning her as the mother of humanity, as the link between the different religious traditions, as the world soul, the mother of creation, the source of all wisdom teachings, as the inspiration behind all conceptions relating to the Divine Feminine, and lastly as the mediating link to universal salvation.

Sophia is the universal mother and the world traditions are her children. She binds them together into one family whose members have been richly bestowed with individual gifts and graces. The relationship between the members of the different world traditions and religions should not be one of opposition but of mutual appreciation and respect. We can learn to appreciate the knowledge of the mystery of God that each religious tradition has to offer. Within the Christian tradition, opening to Sophia implies a willingness to understand that the Logos incarnated into Jesus and the Divine Sophia incarnated into Mary, and that these incarnations are still influencing the work of redemption of humanity and the entire world of nature.

I would like to share a meditation that will help deepen our feeling for Sophia in relation to the Logos and to Mary. This meditation is entitled "Sophia the daughter of God."

In the beginning was Sophia, and Sophia was with God, united with the Logos.
Sophia was in the beginning with God.
All things were made by the Logos and Sophia.
Sophia is wisdom, and wisdom is the light of creation.
And the light shines in the heavens, and the angels radiate it forth.

There was a woman sent from God whose name was Mary. She came for Sophia as bearer of the divine wisdom, that through her the Logos might incarnate into the world. She was illumined by the light of divine wisdom and came to bear the vessel of the Logos. Enlightened by the true Light of heaven she gave birth to Jesus into whom the Logos incarnated. And Sophia took up abode in her. Mary-Sophia was in the world: Sophia through whom, alongside the Logos, the world was created. And the world knew her not. She who delighted in humanity was not received by her own people. But all who receive her now who turn to her as the Daughter of God, she welcomes as sons and daughters of light.

This meditation points to the work of Sophia alongside the Logos from the beginning of the creation, and it refers to the incarnation of Sophia in Mary to help fulfill the work of the Logos in his incarnation into Jesus. Of course, no Christian should feel superior to any believer from any other tradition. It is a matter of coming to an understanding of the harmony between the different world religions, and of grasping how Sophia has worked within the various world religions bringing different aspects of divine wisdom to expression in different places at different times. Now, in our time, we find many enlightened human beings who are receiving the inflowing impulse and message of the Divine Sophia, and it is in accord with the particular tradition, country, time, and place for each person. Such experiences will create harmony, peace, mutual respect, and understanding between all peoples of the Earth and between all religious traditions. We are moving into the Age of Sophia which will enfold all humanity and have its impact upon all people on Earth.

Let me conclude with meditations—first on the etheric Christ, and secondly on Divine Sophia—both drawn from the Book of Revelation. The meditation upon the etheric Christ is found in Chapter 1, in which the Risen Christ appears to John on the island of Patmos. He appears in a radiant form, and nine significant characteristics are described, each pointing to different qualities of the etheric Christ.

Firstly, the etheric Christ has eyes like flames of fire. These eyes glow with the power of divine love, pierce the veil of appearances, and penetrate through to the very core of existence. Secondly, he has hair that is white as snow, like white wool, symbolizing profound wisdom. When we think of a wise sage we tend to think of someone who has attained an advanced age, and the whiteness of the hair portrays this radiance of wisdom. Thirdly, from the mouth of the etheric Christ proceeds a sharp two-edged sword. This is the sword of the Word that can be wielded for the good or against evil. Here we can contemplate the creative power of the Word spoken by the etheric Christ. Fourthly, the face of the Christ shines like the power of the Sun at full strength. This brings to expression again the Sun-filled quality of divine wisdom. Fifth, the voice of the etheric Christ sounds like rushing water, meaning his voice and his entire being are in perfect harmony with all the forces of nature. Sixth, he has a golden girdle around his breast. A golden girdle points to the heartfelt quality of divine love, and shows that all his movements are guided by divine love. Seventh, he is clothed in a long white robe. This symbolizes the transformed will of the Christ, a will that pours outward as the bestowing power of the good. Eighth, the etheric Christ holds seven stars in his right hand. These are the seven stars already mentioned as the seven stages of creation: ancient Saturn, ancient Sun, ancient Moon, present Earth stage of evolution, future Jupiter, future Venus, and future Vulcan. The etheric Christ together with the Divine Sophia watches over humanity and the Earth to guide us through the seven stages of evolution toward its ultimate spiritual goal in the far distant future. Ninth, his feet are like burnished bronze. Here we see the power of divine will streaming through the feet connecting with the Earth, and we might contemplate the image of Christ drawing from the depths of the Divine Mother the force and power that enabled him to walk upon the water. We will also be able to draw regenerating forces from the depths of the Earth through our feet when our level of evolution has purified us enough to sustain this inflow of pure divine life from the Divine Mother. Contemplation of these nine characteristics of the etheric Christ can certainly guide us in our spiritual journey and help to bring us into connection with him.

The meditation on Sophia is drawn from the twelfth chapter of the Book of Revelation, where, as already referred to, Sophia is described as being clothed with the Sun, with the Moon under her feet, and on her head a crown of twelve stars. This image of Sophia as the soul of the world shows her extended body as encompassing all the planets and stars, and from the entire planetary system she pours down her wisdom upon the Earth to those who are open in heart and mind to receive it. Sophia is the archetype for every human soul, and since every human soul is an image of the world soul, Sophia is the ideal for every human soul. This ideal is to become clothed with the Sun, which means to take the light of the spiritual Sun, of the Christ, into our souls, and to become clothed with it. In so doing, our negativity is gradually transformed, and eventually our souls become reunited with the world of stars. The crown of stars points to a future stage of evolution when we will become cosmic beings, united with the whole cosmos, our souls radiating like the Sun, and then the world of the stars will be a crown upon our head.

These two meditations drawn from the Book of Revelation are a helpful guide in our daily spiritual practice to strengthen our connection with Christ and Sophia. Various other prayers and meditations can also assist us in our spiritual journey. I have already referred to the great prayer, the *Our Mother*. When prayed together with the *Our Father* we find the possibility of uniting within ourselves a relationship to the Divine Father in the heights and to the Divine Mother in the depths of the Earth. We are able to balance our masculine and the feminine aspects in order to attain harmony within ourselves. In working with the *Our Father* and the *Our Mother*, an image that may help us is that of a figure eight, where the middle point of this figure eight is to be found in our own hearts. When praying the *Our Father*, we can imagine a stream ascending upwards from our heart toward the transcendental Father of all creation, and that then streaming back as a response of grace from the Father coming back into our heart. Then, in praying the *Our Mother*, the stream goes down toward the depths of the Earth and, once again, we find a response coming this time from the Mother, who sends a stream of divine life up into our hearts. We can be further helped in this contemplation if we think of Christ's descent into the depths of the Earth after his death on the Cross, and of his ascent to the Father in the heights after the resurrection. Here we also see the work of the Christ as the Son of God in uniting the Divine Father and the Divine Mother.

A powerful prayer, which helped to open me to the Virgin Mary as a bearer of Divine Sophia, is the prayer that the Virgin Mary revealed in her apparition in Amsterdam in the year 1951. This is called the *Prayer of the Lady of all Nations* or the *Lady of all Peoples*.

Lord Jesus Christ, Son of the Father,
Send now Thy spirit over the Earth.

Let the Holy Spirit live in the hearts of all peoples,
That they may be preserved from degeneration, disaster, and war.
May the Lady of all peoples, who once was Mary,
Intercede on our behalf.
Amen.

This simple prayer, revealed by the Virgin Mary, is a wonderful prayer for peace on Earth, and peace between all peoples. Standing behind this prayer is the archetypal event of Pentecost when the Holy Spirit descended as tongues of fire upon the disciples who were gathered around the Virgin Mary. During that holy festival of Pentecost, the Virgin Mary became the vessel or the incarnation of Divine Sophia. So the words *Lady of All Peoples, who once was Mary,* point to Divine Sophia who incarnated into Mary at that event two thousand years ago.

This has relevance to a deeper understanding of this prayer for world peace. What took place at the event of Pentecost two thousand years ago? The disciples were transformed into apostles. This meant that they attained a stage of development at which they were no longer learning from the Christ, but were empowered from within to transmit his message. Through the event of Pentecost, the disciples became apostles and went out in all directions of the world to become teachers. This transition from disciple to apostle can take place if one is empowered from above and from within. Divine Sophia plays a significant role in this empowerment.

Due to the consequences of the Fall, including later consequences such as those following the building of the Tower of Babel, we see the diversification of humanity into different nations and different peoples, each speaking a different language. The Divine Sophia is able to build bridges between the different peoples. Sophia can even be pictured as the heart of different folk spirits, or inspirational guides, of the different nations of the world. What this means is that just as every human being has a guardian angel who watches over his or her destiny, so each nation or community of people has an archangel, or folk spirit, who watches and guards over the development of that particular people. The Divine Sophia is able to work on the level of the heart, as the connecting link between all the different peoples of the Earth.

What the apostles experienced through the event of Pentecost was that their souls were elevated into a union with the Divine Sophia. Suddenly, they could understand the different languages that were being spoken. Through Sophia, the apostles had access to all the knowledge of the different tongues of the different peoples. In this way, Sophia works to build a bridge between the different peoples of the Earth. In this sense she is the Queen of Peace among different peoples. This is also the content of the prayer revealed by the Virgin Mary in Amsterdam on February 11, 1951, in her role as the Lady of all Nations:

Lord Jesus Christ, Son of the Father,
Send now Thy spirit over the Earth.
Let the Holy Spirit live in the hearts of all peoples,
That they may be preserved from degeneration, disaster, and war.
May the Lady of all peoples, who once was Mary,
Intercede on our behalf.
Amen.

Here we can understand the Lady of all Peoples as Sophia working in the heart of all the peoples and nations to bring peace to the world. The three prayers—the *Our Father*, the *Our Mother*, and this *Prayer of the Lady of all Peoples*—can be taken as an introduction to the prayer I have described already as the *Little Rosary*, where the *Hail Mary* is recited seven times with the seven divine I AM affirmations of the Christ. The *Little Rosary* builds the heart of this prayer sequence and, if prayed daily, can help us open up to Divine Sophia. Concluding this sequence of prayers, I would like to state the Sophianic expression of the prologue to the Gospel of St. John:

In the beginning was Sophia, and Sophia was with God, united with the Logos.
Sophia was in the beginning with God.
All things were made through the Logos and Sophia.
Sophia is wisdom, and wisdom is the light of creation.
And the light shines in the heavens, and the angels radiate it forth.

This meditative prayer is a great help in focussing our minds and hearts upon Divine Sophia as the bride and companion of Christ, the Logos, in the work of creation, healing, and redemption of humanity. This great work is now at the center of the New Age. Earlier, I referred to the fact that astronomical research shows that the Age of Aquarius will begin in CE 2375, and that we are in the late stages of the present Age of Pisces. Nevertheless this New Age, which began in 1899, and is called Satya Yuga or the Age of Light, can be seen as a preparation leading over into the Age of Aquarius. So this transition to the New Age, which has begun with the twentieth century, is really a time in which we can begin to attune to the Age of Aquarius, which can be called the Age of Sophia, the Age of Universal Wisdom.

Chapter Nine
The Age of Pisces
and the Age of Aquarius

I WOULD LIKE TO END BY REFLECTING MORE ON THE
Age of Pisces, in which we are living, and contrast it with the Age
of Aquarius, which is the coming age. Let us remember that these
astrological ages arise through the phenomenon known in astronomy
as the precession of the equinoxes. This refers to the retrograde
movement of the vernal point backwards through the zodiacal
constellations. The vernal point is defined as the location of the Sun
in the constellations on the day of the vernal equinox which is usually
around March 21. At the present time, the location of the Sun on this
day is around five degrees in the constellation of Pisces. Taking the
average rate of precession to be one degree in seventy-two years each
age lasts 2,160 years, this being the length of time taken for the vernal
point to precess through thirty degrees. 2,160 is thirty multiplied by
seventy-two.

Looking back we find the start of the Age of Pisces around the
year 215 CE. It was exactly at this time in Alexandria that the early

Christians there began to use the symbol of the fish for Jesus Christ. Prior to this time during the Age of Aries, the Christ was referred to as the Lamb of God. As we find in the words of the Gospel of St. John, John the Baptist speaks the words: *Behold the Lamb of God who bears the sins of the world.* The lamb or the ram refers to the constellation of Aries. From the year 215 on with the beginning of the Age of Pisces, Christ began to be referred to as the Divine Fish. There is a deeper background to this. We see that his coming two thousand years ago took place toward the end of the Age of Aries. However, Christ was already preparing during the last part of the Arian Age for the beginning of the Age of Pisces—preparing by drawing his disciples from fishermen and speaking to them as being fishers of human souls. The entire impulse of the Christ at that time was directed toward preparing for the coming Age of Pisces.

In our time, with the Second Coming of Christ, the coming of Christ in an etheric body, the etheric Christ is now working in this last period of the Age of Pisces to prepare for the coming Age of Aquarius. In the words spoken by Christ referring to his second coming, he said: *There will be a time of tribulation and then you will see the sign of the Son of Man in heaven.* In my interpretation of these words, the part of the New Age we are living in now up until the beginning of the Age of Aquarius is the time of tribulation referred to by Jesus Christ. And, moreover, the beginning of the Age of Aquarius, with the entrance of the vernal point into Aquarius, signifies the sign of the Son of Man in heaven.

How can we understand this? The etheric Christ is a being who works in the realm of the life forces, that is the realm to which our own etheric bodies are related. In the Age of Pisces, our consciousness has been brought right down into the physical body. So, in this Age of Pisces, the rise of materialism has been made possible through this intense consciousness of ourselves in a physical body, even to the extent of an identification with the physical body. Pisces, as the zodiacal sign connected with the feet, points to this intense connection with the Earth and with the realm of matter through the feet. The deeper meaning of Christ's "washing of the feet" is that it was a symbolic expression of the need to find a right relationship through the feet with the Earth, a relationship that is pure and unsullied, i.e. untainted by materialism; and this right relationship is particularly important during the Age of Pisces, for which Christ was preparing humanity two thousand years ago.

But this is also the age in which it will be increasingly possible through the feet to find a spiritual relationship with the Divine Mother in the depths of the Earth. Unless we have this spiritual relationship to the Earth in the Age of Pisces, the impulse of materialism will grow stronger and stronger, through this increasing consciousness within the physical body.

In esoteric terms, the etheric body indwelling the physical body and endowing it with life could be called the "waterbearer" in us. The flow of life within us is carried by the watery part of our being. It is this that is imaged in the heavens macrocosmically in the constellation of Aquarius. Aquarius is called the Waterbearer and pours out from the vessel the stream of the waters of life. Therefore, the image of this constellation of the Waterbearer, Aquarius, can be taken as a macrocosmic image of the etheric Christ as the bearer of new life and life forces.

So the entrance of the vernal point into Aquarius can be seen as bringing to realization the prophecy of Christ concerning the appearance of the "sign" of the Son of Man in heaven. I believe this sign is the entrance of the vernal point into Aquarius, and that this will then signify a new consciousness, a transition in consciousness from the physical to the etheric level of existence. In the Age of Aquarius everyone will find that their consciousness will become shifted from the physical level to the etheric level. This means that there will be an awakening to the life forces flowing in nature. There will be an awakening to the flow of life forces in our own being and there will be a direct perception of the etheric body. A new science of healing will arise through this direct perception of how the life forces flow within the physical body, carried by the etheric body. Already now in this New Age, through an attunement to the etheric Christ in this last part of the Age of Pisces, it is possible to begin to enter into this new consciousness that will come to manifestation in the Age of Aquarius. In this sense, the New Age is truly a preparation for the Age of Aquarius.

* * *

As I have suggested, Piscean Age consciousness tends to be focussed on the physical level of existence. This brings with it the tendency to want to possess. So, in this Piscean Age, we speak about *my* car, *my* house, and even *my* wife or *my* husband. This possessive form of relating to the world will dissolve in the Age of Aquarius with the shift of consciousness to the etheric level of existence, where there are not such sharp boundaries as in the physical realm. Therefore, in the Age of Aquarius, there will be much more a feeling for community, a caring for one another, an attunement to each other's needs, and a sensitivity to the other as a free individual.

In our time we can see how there are two distinct divergent tendencies at work in contemporary culture. On the one hand, we are increasingly focussed on the physical body and the physical world, with its attendant materialism. This overemphasis is a negative facet of life in the Piscean Age. On the other hand, there is truly an opening up of spiritual awareness and the development of faculties of the heart—particularly the faculty of intuition, of a direct knowing, a direct awareness through the heart. This precious gift is becoming developed by an increasing number of people in our time. Such an opening of the heart signifies a Sophianic quality that stands in contrast to the will to possess, the will to experience oneself simply as a physical being. Against this background, in the light of the Sophia teachings, I think it is possible to see that there are grave problems in contemporary culture, but that there are solutions that can arise through the spiritual awakening to the true New Age.

By New Age I do not mean a commercialization of spirituality. I mean an awakening to authentic spiritual values of all the true great wisdom traditions of the Earth. This is the best side of what we can call the New Age. This leads toward Aquarian Age consciousness, to new values, to the building of spiritual community, to a completely new relationship to nature and to the whole Earth.

It is this that is now coming about through the event of the return of the etheric Christ and the related event of the descent of Divine Sophia. It is this that can be the central focus for our meditation in the light of the Sophia teachings. Anyone living in the contemporary Western world will recognize the two tendencies I have just described and how they pose a real challenge. These tendencies strike at the heart of the essence of what is taking place in the world at the present time. It is a battle between Christ and Antichrist on the one hand and the battle between Sophia and Antisophia on the other hand. Antisophia is depicted in the Book of Revelation as the great whore of Babylon. It is especially in Western culture that these powerful forces, on the one hand for the good and on the other hand for the negative, are so manifestly at work. Of course, the battle between good and evil is taking place in other cultures as well. The outcome of this battle will influence the whole planet.

Against this background of the dramatic struggle taking place in contemporary culture, the Sophia teachings are highly relevant. At the beginning of this book, we looked at the work of the Divine Sophia opening up the human mind to the inpouring of Divine Wisdom through illumining our power of understanding and expanding our awareness of ourselves in relation to the whole cosmos. This is called *gnosis*, divine knowledge. We also referred to the opening of the heart to Divine Sophia, the opening in love to this extraordinary and wonderful being, as a practice of mystical love with a higher being. When the heart and the mind are opened and aligned with the divine world, it is then possible that our deeds, our alignment of will, can be completely in harmony with the spiritual world. This is called sacred magic.

So, it is with the help of the beings of Christ and Sophia that the deeper mission of awakening spirituality can unfold in this New Age. Our human will can be directed purposefully and in alignment with the intentions of divine wisdom and divine love. This, I would say, is the deeper impact and message of the Sophia teachings for a new spiritual culture, and with this I would like to extend my heartfelt support and hope that all who read this book will be able to find that inner power and strength of spirit to overcome the negative side of modern culture to work for the unfolding of true New Age spirituality—what we can call the spiritual New Age that now wishes to be born in the hearts and minds of everybody who has chosen to incarnate on the Earth at this time. This is the hope for the future—rather than the spread of materialistic culture all around the globe. The spiritual culture of Sophia needs to be born now, in this New Age, and to become a force for the good in the great struggle currently taking place in the entire world. As we begin this new millennium, the Sophia teachings can give inspiration, help, and orientation in the unfolding spiritual impulse of the Divine Feminine.

I would like to close with the final words from Goethe's great drama *Faust*, in which the poet refers to the Eternal Feminine as the guiding power of evolution.

> *Virgin, Mother, Queen,*
> *Keep us, Goddess, in thy grace.*
> *All things corruptible are but a parable*
> *Earth's insufficiency here finds fulfillment.*
> *Here the ineffable wins life through love*
> *The Eternal Feminine leads us above.*

Epilogue

BECAUSE THE TEXT OF *THE SOPHIA TEACHINGS* was transcribed from spoken recordings, notes and references are not included. However, the author recommends the following works containing a number of texts referred to in *The Sophia Teachings*.

Anonymous. *Meditations on the Tarot: A Journey into Christian Hermeticism.* Translated by Robert Powell. New York: Jeremy P. Tarcher/Putnam, 2002.

Powell, Robert A. *Divine Sophia, Holy Wisdom.* Nicasio, CA: The Sophia Foundation of North America, 1997.

——. *The Most Holy Trinosophia and the New Revelation of the Divine Feminine.* Great Barrington, MA: Anthroposophic Press, 2000.

Schipflinger, Thomas. *Sophia Mary: A Holistic Vision of Creation.* Translated by James Morgante. York Beach, ME: Samuel Weiser, 1998.

Tomberg, Valentin. *Covenant of the Heart.* Translated by James Morgante and Robert Powell. Rockport, MA: Element Books, 1992. (Distributed by the Sophia Foundation of North America.)

For further information on the work of the Sophia Foundation of North America, cofounded by Robert Powell and Karen Rivers, please contact:

The Sophia Foundation of North America
3585 Knob Hill Lane
Eugene, OR 97405
Phone/Fax: 541-683-7797
Email: sophia@clipper.net
www.sophiafoundation.org

R+L

L &W

GS

BL

D, E+E

WTL

TV

immanent $\stackrel{?}{=}$ creation